£5.95

MANAGING STRESS

David Fontana

Problems in Practice

This series is the natural successor to the popular *Psychology in Action* series, and continues and extends the aim of 'giving psychology away', that is, making psychological expertise more freely available.

Each title focuses on a common problem across a number of different professions – industry, education, medicine, the police and other public and social services. The approach is practical, drawing on examples from a range of work situations. And the reader is constantly invited to look at the problem both as object and subject: accepting help as well as offering help; dealing with one's own aggressive impulses as well as those directed towards you by others; both giving and requesting expert advice. Psychologists have a great deal to say about how to improve our working lives and the aim here is to offer both practical skills and new insights.

THE AUTHORS AND EDITORS

Glynis Breakwell (Senior Lecturer in Psychology, University of Surrey, Guildford)

David Fontana (Reader in Educational Psychology, University of Wales College of Cardiff)

Glenys Parry (Regional Tutor in Clinical Psychology, Knowle Hospital, Fareham and Top Grade Clinical Psychologist, Department of Psychotherapy, Royal South Hants Hospital, Southampton)

The original, problem-solving approach of this series was applied also to the creation of these titles, by a team of three, acting as both authors and editors. Each member of the team, drawing on their own practical experience, contributed ideas, material and criticism to every title, in addition to taking full responsibility for the writing of at least one of them. This approach ensures a book of wide practical relevance, combining the strengths and expertise of all authors, a uniformity of approach with a minimum of overlap between titles, yet retaining the clear, simple line of the single-authored book. The commitment of the authors to the series made all of this possible.

OTHER TITLES IN THE SERIES

Facing Physical Violence by Glynis Breakwell
Working Through Crises by Glenys Parry
Interviewing by Glynis Breakwell

Problems in Practice

MANAGING STRESS

David Fontana

Reader in Educational Psychology
University of Wales College of Cardiff

Published by The British Psychological Society
and Routledge Ltd.

For my mother

First published in 1989 by The British Psychological Society, St Andrews House, 48 Princess Road East, Leicester, LE1 7DR, in association with Routledge Ltd, 11 New Fetter Lane, London EC4P 4EE, and in the USA by Chapman & Hall Inc., 29 West 35th Street, New York NY 10001.

British Library Cataloguing in Publication Data

Fontana, David
   Managing stress. – (Problems in practice).
   1. Professional personnel. Stress
   I. Title   II. Series
   158.7

ISBN 0–901715–98–0
ISBN 0–901715–97–2 pbk

Printed and bound in Great Britain by Biddles Ltd., Guildford
Whilst every effort has been made to ensure the accuracy of the contents of this publication, the publishers and authors expressly disclaim responsibility in law for negligence or any other cause of action whatsoever.

Contents

Foreword

The stress faced by professional workers is substantial. For many professions, it is intrinsic to the job itself, where competing demands and pressures cannot be escaped. The sheer volume of work can also be overwhelming at times, whether one is a social worker, teacher, doctor or manager. Anyone in this kind of job knows, either from their own direct experience or from observing colleagues, that stress can have very serious consequences. It can develop into a living nightmare of running faster and faster to stay in the same place, feeling under-valued, feeling unable to say 'no' to any demand but not working productively on anything. The signs of stress can include sleeplessness, aches and pains and sometimes physical symptoms of anxiety about going to work. What is more, people who are chronically stressed are no fun to work with. They may be irritable, miserable, lacking in energy and commitment, self-absorbed. They may find it hard to concentrate on any one task and cannot be relied on to do their share.

And yet, some people seem to have the ability to stay in control of their workload and to handle job frustrations without becoming worn out, irritable or depressed. These people are able to handle stress, having ways of taking the rough with the smooth, keeping a sense of humour and renewing their energy and resources so that working life continues to bring pleasure and reward.

David Fontana brings together the many insights offered by a psychological approach to stress. Writing in straightforward, non-technical language, he communicates a wide range of knowledge in a form which the reader can readily assimilate. He offers us not just abstract information, but a really practical guide about the sources of stress and how to deal with them.

This is not 'just another book about stress'. Most books about stress oversimplify the problems faced by professional workers. For example, it is easy to think about stress as if it is 'out there' in the environment and to feel, as individuals, merely victims of external forces. David Fontana does write about these external forces, but, as a psychologist, he knows that whether or not we feel stressed depends not only on circumstances, but also on ourselves. Often we ourselves are the biggest source of stress in our lives. This book is unusual in that it really gets to grips with the role of personality, with how people interpret situations, and with the role of the individual's underlying belief systems in creating and fostering stress. It does this in a way which is optimistic and constructive, showing how we can move to a deeper understanding of ourselves, and giving practical exercises in learning how to do things differently. Of course, we don't like to think that we are partly responsible for our own problems, since it seems much easier to blame the job, the boss, the system. But, as *Managing Stress* demonstrates, we *can* begin to take responsibility for ourselves, and be creative in solving the stress problem.

Glenys Parry and Glynis Breakwell
Series editors

Chapter One

What Is Stress?

Let's start with a little story that was first told by a Zen Master to his students. The story concerns a man (it could just as well be a woman) who is chased by a tiger and falls over a cliff. To break his fall he is lucky enough to catch hold of a small shrub growing on the cliff face, and there he hangs, poised precariously between life and death. Above him the tiger prowls, and looking down he sees another tiger at the cliff bottom. Even were he to survive the fall, there would soon be nothing much left of him to be found by his rescuers. As he hangs there, he sees two small mice busily gnawing away at the stem of the shrub on which his life depends. Simultaneously he sees some wild strawberries growing just within reach, plucks them and pops them into his mouth and thinks to himself, 'Ah how sweet these strawberries taste!'

I suppose it's probable that the poor fellow plunged to his untimely death long before he had a chance to share his secret with other mortals, but even if he can't tell us how he remained so serene, at least he's a perfect example of being unstressed in stressful circumstances. He had time to take delight in the taste of the wild strawberries, even with the shock of being chased by a tiger fresh in his mind and the awful prospect of being dashed and gored to pieces lying just ahead. I shall return to the story later in the book, because it exemplifies clearly one of the main messages of this book, namely that in the final analysis, it isn't external events, however hectic or unpleasant, that determine whether we're stressed or not; it's something inside ourselves.

WHAT IS STRESS?

It isn't easy to find a generally acceptable definition of 'stress'. The word is used loosely, with different people and different groups of people taking it to mean different things. Doctors, engineers, psychologists, management consultants, linguists and laypeople all use the word in their own distinctive ways. Doctors talk in terms of physiological mechanisms, engineers in terms of load bearing, psychologists in terms of behaviour change, management consultants in terms of organisational challenge, linguists in terms of syllable emphasis and laypeople in terms of almost anything under the sun, from the complexities of balancing the household budget to parents stressing certain do's and don'ts to their children. Some people suggest that stress is natural and even desirable (engineers, linguists) others that it's something we suffer from (doctors and laypeople).

Let's try to clarify things a little by looking at the origin of the word. It seems to have come into the English language (via Middle English) from the Old French word *destresse*, which meant to be placed under narrowness or oppression (Old French *estresse*). In its Middle English form it was therefore 'distress', and it is only over the centuries that the 'di' sometimes got lost through slurring, leaving us with two words 'stress' and 'distress', which have now come to carry rather different meanings, the one ambivalent, the second always indicating something unpleasant.

In terms of its origins, therefore, 'stress' has to do with constriction or oppression of some kind, and 'distress' the state of being under this constriction or oppression. But Modern English seems to need a word that lies partway between 'pressure' and 'emphasis', carrying something of the potentially painful connotations of the former and something of the more neutral connotations of the latter, and with the course of time 'stress' has become that word.

In the technical literature the consensus, such as it is, seems to be towards defining stress in the pressure/emphasis way, rather than in the constriction/oppression way, and that's the approach I shall adopt in this book. The significance of this is that the word (and the real-life experiences that it represents) can be seen as neither good nor bad *in itself*. Before judging it, we have to take into account the context in which it occurs. At one end of the scale, stress represents those challenges which excite us and keep us on our toes, and without which life for many people would become dull and ultimately not worth living. At the other end of the scale, stress represents those conditions under which individuals have demands made upon them that they cannot physically or psychologically meet, and that lead to breakdown at one or other of these levels. At one end of the scale, therefore, stress is a life-saver, at the other a life-destroyer. To understand it and how it works, we must keep both ends of the scale firmly in mind.

So now to a snappy definition that will encapsulate this multi-faceted word. The one I'm going to adopt is that *stress is a demand made upon the adaptive capacities of the mind and body*. If these capacities can handle the demand and enjoy the stimulation involved, then stress is welcome and helpful. If they can't and find the demand debilitating, then stress is unwelcome and unhelpful. This definition is useful in three ways. Firstly it makes clear not only that stress can be both good or bad (or somewhere in between), but that since there is a very wide range of things that can make demands upon the mind and body (from the neighbourhood children ringing the doorbell and running away to the threatened outbreak of World War III) there is a very wide range of things that can cause stress (*stressors*). Secondly it infers the point that I made after recounting the Zen story, namely that it isn't so much events that determine whether we're stressed or not, as our reactions to them. And thirdly the definition tells us that stress is a *demand* made upon the body's '*capacities*'. It is the nature and extent of these capacities (i.e. something inside ourselves) that determine our response to the demand. If our capacities are good enough, we respond well. If they aren't, we give way.

IDENTIFYING EXTERNAL DEMANDS AND PERSONAL CAPACITIES

So if we want to understand stress, we must look both at external demands (what are they, and how can they be increased or lessened as required?) and at our personal capacities (how do we react to stress, and how can our reactions be modified as necessary?). We must also recognise right at the outset that just as demands can vary from situation to situation, so capacities can vary from person to person. Or even within the same person from one year or month or day to the next. Suspended over the cliff with hungry tigers above and below and with energetic mice nibbling busily through our life support system, most of us would be screaming our heads off. But just occasionally one of us might be reaching out for a wild strawberry and savouring it with a smile on our lips.

Whether we fall within the first or second category will depend upon a number of factors, both inherited and learnt, and I'll be discussing them all later in the book. But clearly we can talk in terms of a desirable equilibrium within each individual between the strength of demand and the capacity to respond. If demand is way below capacity, we may feel bored and under-stimulated (which can produce psychological and physical problems just as damaging as those produced by stress). If demand is way above capacity, we may feel over-stretched and eventually overwhelmed. Where such over-stretching takes place, we can either try reducing the demand until it falls within the limits of existing capacities, or we can try increasing these capacities until they meet the existing levels of demand. Or we can try simultaneously both to reduce demand and to increase capacities, until the two achieve an acceptable degree of harmony.

In practical terms, what this means is that any person under stress must look firstly at the *environment*, to identify the demands that are being made upon him or her and to see whether these demands can be altered or lessened in any way, and secondly at *him or herself* to see whether personal reactions to these demands can be similarly modified, thus either increasing capacity or making better use of what capacity is already available.

Conversely, if we are bored or under-stimulated, it means we must identify how more demands can be made upon us by the environment, and how we can increase our capacity to be stimulated by such demands as we already have. In the book, I shall concentrate primarily upon those cases where the demands of the environment outstrip capacity to respond, but we mustn't lose sight of the fact that under-stressing can be as bad in its way as over-stressing, and from time to time I shall touch upon this aspect of things as well.

Stress is a natural and unavoidable feature of life. In underdeveloped communities, stressors can be related primarily to the need for physical survival, to finding food and shelter for example, to finding safety and a mate to procreate the species. In developed cultures (especially those of the modern Western world) our stressors have usually rather less to do with the basic mechanics of survival, and rather more to do with social success, with the generation of ever-increasing standards of living, and with meeting the expectations of ourselves and others. Whether modern 'unnatural' stressors put more pressure on us than the stressors we faced in more basic times is a matter for debate.

But the point is that stressors seem such a natural part of the human condition that if they aren't there of their own accord we make a pretty good job of inventing them for ourselves. The simplest example of this at the individual level is the way in which we put ourselves under pressure by leaving things to the last moment. Not just the unpleasant things that we'd rather not do anyway, but even the pleasant things that we enjoy doing or that are necessary if we're to feel fulfilled and valued. It seems that many of us can only do our best work when we experience this pressure, like the great French novelist Balzac, who wrote only when he had first piled up mountains of debt.

There may also be an element in some people of enjoying putting *others* under stress, and this is something that has to be considered when developing strategies for dealing with colleagues and superiors at work. Acting as a stressor for others may enhance an individual's sense of power and personal prestige. Or it may simply appeal to the sadist in him or her, however much they may try and rationalise it away with talk of maintaining standards and 'getting the best' out of people.

WHAT HAPPENS WHEN DEMANDS OUTSTRIP CAPACITY?

We can answer this question at two levels, the physiological and the psychological. As this is a practical book, I won't dwell too long on physiological issues, but something needs to be said about them if we're to understand the harmful consequences of too much stress. And since medical opinion estimates that between a half and three quarters of all illnesses and accidents are excess-stress related, there's little doubt that these consequences are often very harmful indeed. In view of the way that mind and body apparently influence each other, we also can't usefully separate physiological issues entirely from psychological ones. So let's look briefly at what happens to body mechanics when stress goes beyond the optimum level, before we turn to more visible behavioural factors.

PHYSIOLOGICAL CONSEQUENCES OF TOO MUCH STRESS

Each of the body's reactions to stress demands is useful in and of itself. They gear the body up to respond to the challenges facing it, either by standing ground and hitting back or by a prompt strategic withdrawal. This so-called 'fight or flight' response happens at the autonomic nervous level. That is, we don't will it consciously through the central nervous system. It happens automatically, in the same way in which the body handles such things as digestion, or raises the heart rate when we run for a bus, or adjusts our bodily thermostat when we move from a warm room to a cold room or vice versa. We don't have any say in the matter. The body recognises the need for a response, and produces it without our having to tell it to do so.

In the course of this response, a range of things happen within the body, each fulfilling a specific role in gearing us up to meet the challenge in front of us. The problem is, however, that each of these things can damage the body if it's allowed to go on for too long. They're each intended by nature as an immediate, short-term reaction, designed to shut down again as soon as the emergency is past. If they don't shut down, they begin to have an adverse effect. Rather like a citizen army which is mobilised to meet an external threat, and which then stays mobilised without being allowed to go into battle as intended. Not only does the country suffer because its citizens put their energy into bearing arms instead of tending the crops and running the economy, it also suffers because the unoccupied soldiery get restless and destructive, pillaging the countryside and getting up to all kinds of illegal practice. The country is siphoning off its lifeblood to defend itself, only to have that lifeblood turn against it.

The human body has evolved over thousands of years to meet external threats by mobilising and then standing down, but the environment in which we now live has changed to such an extent since the Industrial Revolution that, once mobilised, our army is neither able to fulfil its brief for fight or flight, nor to be sure that danger is passed and stand down. Our modern society doesn't usually allow us *physically* to fight or run away when we face stressors, nor does it remove these stressors so that we're allowed to relax. We remain in a constant state of preparedness for action which we aren't permitted to take, and the body after a while begins to feel the effects. Many thousands of years hence, perhaps, human physiology will have evolved beyond the fight–flight response, and produced something capable of adapting as necessary to the actual demands that life makes upon it. But for the present, we're using a system developed over millions of years of living close to nature, to cope with an environment which has changed out of all recognition in little over a century. No wonder the system has a tendency to break down.

It's useful to look at the main aspects of the body's response to stress, and the damage each of these can inflict if allowed to go on too long. For convenience I group these aspects under the four subheadings below, but in practice they're all closely interrelated (for example the release of adrenalin, mentioned under the first subheading, is responsible for prompting many of the effects mentioned under the other three).

ENERGY MOBILISERS

The energy mobilisers, to continue our military analogy, are the front-line troops, the ones who provide the instant energy needed for fight or flight. They provoke the following effects:

✓ *Release into the bloodstream of adrenalin and noradrenalin from the adrenal glands.* These act as powerful stimulants, speeding up reflexes, increasing heart rate and blood pressure, raising blood sugar levels, and raising bodily metabolism. The result is increased short-term capacity and performance, as more blood is carried to the muscles and to the lungs, energy supplies are boosted, and responses sharpened.

✗ *But* if all this isn't translated into instant action, long-term consequences can include cardiovascular disorders such as heart disease and strokes, kidney damage due to raised blood pressure, and disturbance of blood sugar levels thus aggravating diabetes and hypoglycaemia.

✓ *Release into the bloodstream of thyroid hormones from the thyroid gland.* These further boost bodily metabolism, thus increasing the rate at which energy can be burnt and translated into physical activity.

✗ *But* allowed to go on too long, this racing metabolism leads to exhaustion, weight loss, and eventual physical collapse.

✓ *Release into the bloodstream of cholesterol from the liver.* This gives a further boost to energy levels, aiding muscle function.

✗ *But* permanently elevated blood cholesterol levels correlate with a greatly increased risk of arteriosclerosis (hardening of the arteries), a major factor in heart disease and heart attacks.

ENERGY SUPPORT SYSTEMS

In addition to the mobilisation of energy itself, there are a number of bodily functions mustered in response to stress which assist this mobilisation. These are analogous to the support troops just behind the front line, who assist the frontline troops in their duties.

✓ *Shut down of digestive system.* This allows blood to be diverted from the stomach so that it can be put to use in the lungs and muscles.

At the same time the mouth goes dry, so that the stomach doesn't even have the task of dealing with saliva.

✗ *But* the shutdown of the digestion, if prolonged, can lead to stomach troubles and digestive upsets, particularly when we force food into the unwilling system.

✓ *Skin reaction.* Blood is diverted from the surface of the skin for use elsewhere (hence the pallor characteristic of those under deep stress), while simultaneously sweat is produced to help cool muscles overheated by the sudden inrush of energy.

✗ *But* the skin needs its blood supply if it is to remain healthy, and excessive sweating is not only antisocial, it also looses valuable body heat (which takes energy to replace) and upsets the body's natural thermostat.

✓ *Air passages in lungs dilate.* This allows the blood to take up more oxygen, a process assisted by an increased breathing rate.

✗ *But* super-oxygenated blood can lead to blackouts and upset heart rhythms.

CONCENTRATION AIDS

These are rather like the staff officers behind the lines who keep the troops focused on the job in hand and eliminate unwanted distractions.

✓ *Release into the bloodstream of endorphins from the hypothalamus.* These act as natural painkillers, and reduce sensitivity to bodily injuries such as bruises and wounds.

✗ *But* when endorphines are depleted, this leaves us *more* sensitive to routine aches and pains such as headaches and backaches.

✓ *Release into the bloodstream of cortisone from the adrenal glands.* This shuts down allergic reactions which could interfere with breathing etc.

✗ *But* this lowers the body's immune reactions to all kinds of infection (and perhaps even cancer), and may increase the risk of peptic ulcers. And once the immediate effects wear off, allergic reactions can return with increased force (as for example when asthma attacks worsen under stress).

 Senses become more acute and mental performance improves, producing enhanced short-term functioning.

✗ *But* above a certain limit or if prolonged too long, these effects go into reverse, actively depressing sensory and mental responses.

 Sex hormone production reduces. This avoids the diversion of energy or attention to sexual arousal, and reduces the potential distractions consequent upon pregnancy and childbirth.

✗ *But* when prolonged the reduction can lead to impotency, frigidity, sterility and other sex problems.

DEFENSIVE REACTIONS

Finally, like the troops back at the base, action is taken to limit the damage done by enemy offensives.

 Blood vessels constrict and blood thickens, so that it flows less rapidly and coagulates more quickly in the event of flesh wounds.

✗ *But* the heart has to work much harder to force this sludge through the narrowed arteries and veins, increasing both the load placed upon it and the chances of blood clots forming, thus boosting the risk of heart disease and strokes.

I hope this sorry catalogue of self-inflicted injuries doesn't make you too depressed. The intention is simply to alert you to the physical dangers of living for any length of time under too much stress, and to the necessity for doing something about this stress if it's there. And if I've now stressed you further by giving the impression that since they're controlled by the autonomic rather than the central nervous system you can't reduce these physical dangers, let me reassure you. Although we may not be able to do anything directly about our autonomic responses (at least not without specialised training), we *can* learn how to stop giving our body the kinds of signal that prompt the autonomic system into activity. I'll return to this in later chapters, but it wouldn't be fair to leave it without a single example.

Let's suppose you invariably arrive home from work in the evenings before any of the rest of the family. One night you arrive as usual and let yourself into what you take to be a deserted house (it helps the story if we imagine the house to be rather old and rambling). Suddenly you hear footsteps in one of the empty rooms above your head, and next moment the footsteps start descending the stairs. Immediately the autonomic responses are switched on at full strength, and gear you up to do battle with the intruder or (in my case at least) to get back out of the house as fast as your legs can carry you. However, a moment later the owner of the footsteps turns the bend in the stairs, and proves to be your wife, husband or some other family member. There has been a quite unexpected change in his or her schedule at work, which means finishing an hour earlier and so always being home first in future. Next night when you enter the house and hear the same footsteps, you're able to switch off the autonomic response before it's even got started, simply by reassuring yourself that far from presenting you with a threat they're actually a welcome sound.

The point about this example is that the external event (the sound of the footsteps) is exactly the same on both occasions. What is different is your mental interpretation· (or *cognitive appraisal*) of it, and it is this cognitive appraisal that often triggers or fails to trigger the autonomic response. You don't usually directly select this response ('Okay I've decided to be really frightened about this'), nor do you instruct the adrenal glands and the thyroid and the liver and all the other agencies to go about their work. But nevertheless it's your appraisal of the footsteps as either threatening or non-threatening that calls up or doesn't call up your citizen army. As we shall see in due course, some individuals have citizen armies which are mustered at the least little sign of threat, while others have armies which require a full-scale war to make them take up their weapons. There are probably both temperamental and learnt reasons for this. But everyone's reactions at the cognitive level (the level of thinking and knowing) have an influence upon what happens at the physiological level, so by changing these reactions where possible we can help damp down unwanted autonomic activity.

PSYCHOLOGICAL CONSEQUENCES OF TOO MUCH STRESS

I've already said that certain levels of stress seem psychologically beneficial to us. They add interest to life, put us on our toes, help us think quicker and work more intensively, and encourage us to feel useful and valued, with a definite purpose to our lives and definite objectives to attain. When stress goes beyond optimum levels however, it drains our psychological energy, impairs our performance, and often leaves us feeling useless and undervalued, with diminishing purpose and hopeless, unattainable objectives. The late Hans Selye, who did much to focus the attention of the medical profession and of psychologists upon the effects of stress, popularised the *general adaptation syndrome* (GAS) model of our reaction to stressors. This recognises three phases in our response, namely:

A. *the alarm reaction*

B. *the stage of resistance*

C. *the stage of exhaustion*

Originally a biological model, these three phases illustrate what we have just been saying about physiological responses to stress. The body is alerted (alarm reaction), autonomic activity is triggered (the stage of resistance), and if this activity goes on too long damage is done and collapse occurs (the stage of exhaustion). Diagrammatically, these phases are sometimes shown as follows:

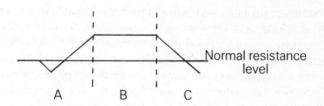

The three phases of the general adaptation syndrome

The small dip during phase A, the alarm reaction, indicates that on first exposure to a stressor physiological resistance actually decreases briefly, while the body summons its forces (the citizen army) for resistance. The duration of phase B, the stage of resistance, very much depends upon the strength of the individual, but if it is forced to continue for too long, phase C, the stage of exhaustion, invariably follows.

This biological model is also useful when considering psychological issues. On facing a stressor, there is usually a pause (long or short depending upon the immediacy and the complexity respectively of the stressor) while the individual makes his or her cognitive appraisals. Once made, there is a stage of resistance (of coping) with the stressor, followed (if prolonged beyond the individual's capacity to hold out) by a stage of psychological collapse. During the stage of resistance, psychological functioning may be enhanced, during the stage of descent from resistance to collapse it will be progressively impaired, and once collapse is reached it may cease to function usefully at all.

Due to the close links between physiology and psychology, physiological phases A B and C may map almost exactly onto psychological phases A B and C for the majority of people. Physiological and psychological energy are not distinct from each other. The more drained we feel physically by stress, the more drained we feel psychologically, and vice versa. But a few individuals give up psychologically as soon as they feel the first signs of physiological toll, while at the other extreme a few keep going up to and even beyond the stage of physical collapse, driving themselves on by what we call willpower alone.

In terms of the beneficial or harmful *psychological* effects of stress, the former apply up to a certain point during phase B, the resistance phase (the exact point depending upon the individual's cognitive appraisals of the usefulness of the stressor, and on his or her powers of resistance and need for challenge), and the latter then take over and hold sway up to and through phase C, the exhaustion phase. These harmful effects vary from individual to individual, but the most important of them can be summarised as shown below. I have divided them into effects to do with thinking and knowing (*cognitive effects*), effects to do with feelings, emotions and personality (*emotional effects*), and effects that call equally upon cognitive and affective factors (*general behavioural effects*). But the three divisions overlap at a number of points, and their use is for practical convenience rather than for academic precision.

COGNITIVE EFFECTS OF TOO MUCH STRESS

- CONCENTRATION AND ATTENTION SPAN DECREASE

  The mind finds it hard to remain focused. Powers of observation diminish.

- DISTRACTABILITY INCREASES

  The thread of what is being thought or said is frequently lost, even in mid-sentence.

- SHORT- AND LONG-TERM MEMORY DETERIORATE

  Memory span reduces. Recall and recognition even of familiar material decline.

- RESPONSE SPEED BECOMES UNPREDICTABLE

  Actual response speed reduces; attempts to compensate may lead to hurried, snap decisions.

- ERROR RATE INCREASES

As a result of all the above, errors increase in manipulative and cognitive tasks. Decisions become suspect.

- POWERS OF ORGANISATION AND LONG-TERM PLANNING DETERIORATE

The mind cannot accurately assess existing conditions or forecast future consequences.

- DELUSIONS AND THOUGHT DISORDERS INCREASE

Reality testing becomes less efficient, objectivity and critical powers are reduced, thought patterns become confused and irrational.

EMOTIONAL EFFECTS OF TOO MUCH STRESS

- PHYSICAL AND PSYCHOLOGICAL TENSIONS INCREASE

The ability to relax muscle tone, to feel good, to switch off worries and anxiety, reduces.

- HYPOCHONDRIA INCREASES

Imagined complaints are added to the real stress maladies. Feelings of health and well-being disappear.

- CHANGES TAKE PLACE IN PERSONALITY TRAITS

Neat and careful people may become untidy and slipshod, caring people indifferent, democratic people authoritarian.

- EXISTING PERSONALITY PROBLEMS INCREASE

Existing anxiety, over-sensitivity, defensiveness and hostility all worsen.

- MORAL AND EMOTIONAL CONSTRAINTS WEAKEN

Codes of behaviour and sex-impulse control weaken (or conversely may become unrealistically rigid). Emotional outbursts increase.

- DEPRESSION AND HELPLESSNESS APPEAR

Spirits sink lower, a sense of powerlessness to influence

events or one's feelings about
them and oneself emerges.

● SELF-ESTEEM FALLS SHARPLY

Feelings of incompetence and
worthlessness develop.

GENERAL BEHAVIOURAL EFFECTS OF TOO MUCH STRESS

● SPEECH PROBLEMS INCREASE

Existing stammering, stuttering
and hesitancy increase, and
may appear in hitherto
unaffected people.

● INTERESTS AND ENTHUSIASMS
DIMINISH

Objectives and life-goals may
be abandoned. Hobbies may be
dropped. Cherished
possessions may be disposed
of.

● ABSENTEEISM INCREASES

Through real or imagined
illness, or manufactured
excuses, lateness or absence
from work become a problem.

● DRUG ABUSE INCREASES

Alcohol, caffeine, nicotine,
prescribed or illegal drug taking
become more evident.

● ENERGY LEVELS ARE LOW

Energy levels drop, or may
fluctuate markedly from day to
day for no obvious reason.

● SLEEP PATTERNS ARE
DISRUPTED

Difficulty getting to sleep or
staying asleep for more than
about four hours at a time
occurs.

● CYNICISM ABOUT CLIENTS AND
COLLEAGUES INCREASES

The tendency develops to lay
the blame upon others – 'What
can you do with people like
that?' 'They'll only be in the
same fix again in six months'.
'Nobody bothers except me'.

● NEW INFORMATION IS IGNORED

Even potentially very helpful
new regulations or new

developments are rejected –
'I'm far too busy to bother with
things like that'.

- RESPONSIBILITIES ARE SHIFTED
  ONTO OTHERS

The tendency to redraw
boundaries, excluding
unpalatable duties from one's
own province, increases.

- PROBLEMS ARE 'SOLVED' AT AN
  INCREASINGLY SUPERFICIAL
  LEVEL

Stop-gap and short-term
solutions are adopted.
Attempts to dig deep or to
follow-up are abandoned. In
some areas, 'giving up' occurs.

- BIZARRE BEHAVIOUR PATTERNS
  APPEAR

Odd mannerisms,
unpredictability,
uncharacteristic behaviour
emerge.

- SUICIDE THREATS MAY BE
  MADE

Phrases such as 'end it all',
'pointless going on' appear.

Let me repeat that the incidence of these adverse effects will vary from
individual to individual. Very few people, even under the most
extreme stress, will show them all; the degree of severity will also vary
from person to person. But the appearance of these symptoms indicates that the individual has reached or is on the way to reaching the
collapse phase of the general adaptation syndrome. If you recognise
any of them in yourself (I'm not counting the initial tendency we many
of us have when reading through lists of medical or psychological
symptoms to conclude grimly that we've got them all!), it could be a
danger sign. I'll give further help in the recognition of danger signs in
the next chapter, and then we'll go on to discuss what causes these
symptoms and what you can do to cope with these causes.

DRUGS FOR STRESS

Drugs to combat stress include not just prescription drugs from the doctor's surgery (sleeping pills, tranquillisers) but also alcohol, nicotine, and the caffeine in tea, coffee and cola. Intake of these drugs often increases sharply as the pressures of life mount. *All* of them are addictive, and in the case of many prescription drugs, as well as alcohol and nicotine, the addiction often results in both physical and psychological damage. Even caffeine can kill. There are only two golden rules when using a stress-reducing drug. Firstly, use it in strict moderation. And secondly, stop using it altogether the moment you realise you are becoming dependent upon it to feel good.

▶ STRICT MODERATION. The intake of prescription drugs is laid down for you by the doctor, but in the case of alcohol, strict moderation means no more than three measures of an alcoholic drink per day for men and two for women. (A measure is a glass of wine, or a single tot of spirits or a half pint of beer.) Above this amount, and both physical and psychological damage may occur. Below or at this amount, and alcohol has a useful role in helping relaxation and may also reduce the risk of heart disease. The French, whose daily intake of alcohol is notoriously high, have only one third the incidence of heart disease of the British (this is the good alcoholic news), but they have a much higher incidence of strokes and of cirrhosis of the liver (this is the bad).

For tea or cola, the limit is four cups or glasses a day. The body stores caffeine, and above this amount poisonous effects can become evident. In the case of coffee, even this limit isn't safe. Some experts consider that a link between even mild coffee intake and a higher incidence of heart disease has been established.

There is no safe limit for smoking. Rates for lung cancer and heart disease are higher even amongst non-smokers if they are exposed consistently to a smoky atmosphere.

▶ DEPENDENCY UPON DRUGS FOR GOOD FEELINGS. Good feelings don't come out of a pill bottle (or even a wine bottle). At best, drugs provide only a temporary high, followed by a low. If you're habitually in poor spirits due to stress, the answer, as emphasised throughout this book, is to deal with the *causes of stress in the environment* and *your own responses to them.*

Chapter Two

How Stressed Are You?

The picture that emerges from the last chapter of the over-stressed man or woman is that of a wretched individual, blood loaded with dangerous chemicals, digestion shot to pieces, skin grey and clammy, sleepless, irrational, moody, alcoholic, sexually incapable and with worse concentration than a butterfly, cowering behind a pill-strewn desk in a disorganised pretence of an office.

But even in the event of all these symptoms coming together (and I've said this is unlikely), this picture may be far from the truth, since many people are adept at hiding their stress, from themselves as well as from everyone else. In the case of professionals with heavy responsibilities for decision making and for controlling the lives of others, this can be a very dangerous state of affairs. Colleagues may be aware that their judgement in important matters is now highly suspect, but little or nothing can be proved, and the individuals concerned may go on in their posts until they cause a real disaster or until their health breaks down mentally or physically.

A contributory problem is that organisations and the people within them are still often reluctant to take the problem of undue stress seriously. In spite of the well-attested physiological and psychological damage I've just summarised, many of those at managerial level or in the caring professions take an admission that you're cracking under pressure as a sign that you're either not up to the job or that you're a malingerer. And many of those affected by stress take the same view. To admit you can't take the pressure is a sign of weakness in yourself, so at all costs you must hang on, whatever the ultimate consequences both for the job which you're struggling hard to do and for your own mind and body (to say nothing of your relationship with colleagues and family and friends).

Jennifer: a case study of unrecognised stress

❏ Jennifer is a 42-year-old schoolteacher, with six years' experience in the classroom. She qualified as a mature student, having waited until her third and youngest child was at infant school before enrolling on a one-year postgraduate course of teacher training. As a physics teacher, she quickly found herself in a senior post in a large comprehensive school, taking responsibility for GCE A-Level work and for much of the fifth-form examination work as well. In the 20 years since she took her physics degree, the subject has advanced considerably, and what little leisure time she has after marking work, preparing lessons and looking after her young family is spent·trying to keep up to date. Husband Keith, a civil engineer, is site manager for a large construction company, and is frequently away from home for sizeable periods of time. Since starting teaching, Jennifer has noticed that she always seems to be tired. She sleeps badly, often sitting up into the early hours of the morning ('the only time when I can get a little peace and quiet' she claims) over her school work. She notices that it is harder and harder to relax at the end of the school day, and is concerned by her failure to remember the facts and figures associated with her work and even human details like children's names. She worries that she seems to be neglecting her family, and snapping habitually at her own children over minor issues. The vague aches and pains that afflict her most of the time, together with the poor digestion and the breathlessness and palpitations, she puts down vaguely to her 'time of life'. She has tried several times to discuss her workload with her head of department and with her head teacher, but they rarely have time to listen, and have told her she should be better organised, plan her lessons more carefully, and attend more refresher courses during the school holidays to keep herself up to date. When she's mentioned her problems to her colleagues, they say they feel exactly the same as she does, and quickly change the subject. She confesses to being angry with herself for not staying more on top of her job, and guilty for all the things she leaves undone both at school and at home.

It's clear that Jennifer can't go on much longer under this sort of strain. It's also clear that she's getting no kind of support from those around

— WHAT JENNIFER SHOULD DO —

Jennifer is part of that vast army of people who in the middle years of life are working too long and too hard. She has nobody with whom she can discuss her situation, and no clear ideas on how she can make her life easier. There are ways in which she can reduce both the stress caused by her environment and by her reactions to her environment, and these are the subjects of later chapters. But without delay Jennifer should:

❏ *Assess realistically what she can and cannot expect of herself.* We assume our capacities are limitless. They're not. Jennifer's husband is away much of the time and can give her little help. She has a responsible, full-time job, three school-age children, a home to run, and she isn't getting any younger. She must clarify what she *can* do, and stop feeling guilty for the things she *can't*.

❏ *Let others know her limitations.* Husband, school and children must be told clearly what these limits are. Jennifer must put them in writing, and give appropriate copies to each of these three parties (the children's copy can be prominently displayed on the kitchen wall). People will go on taking advantage of Jennifer until she asserts herself. It's a sad fact that the less fuss we make the more others take us for granted.

❏ *Earmark some time each day which is her own.* Jennifer's life is spent servicing others. It's unacceptable that the only time she has to herself is late at night.

❏ *Arrange a proper meeting with colleagues to discuss stress.* Jennifer gets little support from her colleagues because she talks to them in a vague, disorganised way. If they're as stressed as they claim, they'll welcome the chance of a proper meeting where they can share their problems.

her. She carries a heavy load at school and the main burden of the work at home, yet blames herself for most of what's going wrong, and has a rapidly deteriorating sense of her own value. Unless things change, she's unlikely to have another six years ahead of her in the teaching profession.

ASSESSING YOUR STRESS LEVEL

You may not feel that you have much in common with Jennifer, but often stress creeps up on you. We're all familiar with single, sudden stressful events, such as moving house or changing jobs or being held up by traffic on the way to an important meeting. What we're not so conscious of is the stress that gradually accumulates, like a screw given a quarter turn every few days or so, from a job which inexorably acquires more responsibilities, or a timetable that gets that little bit tighter, or a workload that keeps having new bits added on, or a mind and body that grow older and are less able to handle demands that at one time we would have taken in our stride. Or a turnover amongst our superiors or colleagues that erodes the number of people with whom we can discuss our problems or to whom we can turn if we want a little unscheduled help with what we're doing.

There are a number of stress scales in existence that ask you to tick whether certain things apply to you or not, and then add up your score at the end. A score above a certain level shows for example that you're 'slightly stressed', higher still and you're 'moderately stressed' and so on. The problem with such scales is that although the adverse consequences of too much stress are similar for most people, *their reactions to them* can be very different. To take an instance, absenteeism increases generally when people are over-stressed, but some individuals show an actual *decrease* in absenteeism, forcing themselves to go into work even when they're genuinely unwell, either through a need to drive and 'prove' themselves or through a fear that decisions unfavourable to them will be taken if they're not around to protect their interests. Thus a question on a stress scale designed to assess whether your absenteeism has increased may produce misleading answers.

Another problem is that stress levels don't necessarily remain constant. If you complete a stress scale when things are going well, you may produce a different score from the one you get when things are going badly. The circumstances within which stress occurs also vary from individual to individual, depending upon the kind of job they do and the way in which they interpret their professional role. Stress can also sometimes be related to specific irritations, like an unpopular boss. When he or she is away, the atmosphere improves dramatically. And finally there's the 'yes but' response which most people feel when faced with stress scales. '*Yes* I feel like that some of the time, *but* not always.' '*Yes* that happens in one area of my work, *but* not in others'. '*Yes* I sometimes worry about that, *but* other times I just laugh about it'. Faced with the 'yes but' syndrome, many people say they want to qualify most of their answers to stress scale items. And two people looking at identical scores after completing a scale will often disagree with each other over whether they feel stressed or not. One does, the other doesn't.

The following stress scale must be treated as a useful guide rather than as a precise instrument therefore. Complete it quickly, and don't think too hard before responding to each question. Your first response is often the most accurate one. As with any stress scale, it isn't difficult to spot what is the 'low stress' answer to each question. Don't be tempted to give this answer if it isn't the accurate one. Nothing is at stake. *You are as stressed as you are.* Your score on the scale doesn't change that, one way or the other. The purpose of the scale is simply to help you clarify some of your thinking about your own life.

IDENTIFYING PATTERNS OF STRESS

Having completed the scale, you will also find it helpful to look back over the effects of stress summarised under the three headings on pages 12–15 and ask yourself whether there's a general pattern there that applies to you. The pattern may extend across the three areas represented by the headings, or it may be confined predominantly to one or two. You may feel that some of the general effects and affective effects apply to you for example, but not the cognitive ones. You feel emotionally pressurised, but still think with your usual sharpness. For a time, with the adrenalin flowing, you may even feel that you're thinking better than ever. On the other hand you may have a feeling that you *are* making more mistakes than usual, and find it harder to keep focused on what you're doing and make plans for the future, but that you're not experiencing any extreme emotional upset.

Alternatively, you may find that identifying a pattern in one area makes you look rather more closely at the other two, and helps you to see that after all yes, there are some things there that apply to you. Or you may feel that just one effect in one area is very marked, but this nevertheless sets you thinking about your life in general. A typical example is the loss of interests and enthusiasms, mentioned under

PROFESSIONAL LIFE STRESS SCALE

1. Two people who know you well are discussing you. Which of the following statements would they be most likely to use?

   (a) 'X is very together. Nothing much seems to bother him/her.'

   (b) 'X is great. But you have to be careful what you say to him/her at times.'

   (c) 'Something always seems to be going wrong with X's life.'

   (d) 'I find X very moody and unpredictable.'

   (e) 'The less I see of X the better!'

2. Are any of the following common features of your life?
   - Feeling you can seldom do anything right
   - Feelings of being hounded or trapped or cornered
   - Indigestion
   - Poor appetite
   - Difficulty in getting to sleep at night
   - Dizzy spells or palpitations
   - Sweating without exertion or high air temperature
   - Panic feelings when in crowds or in confined spaces
   - Tiredness and lack of energy
   - Feelings of hopelessness ('what's the use of anything?')
   - Faintness or nausea sensations without any physical cause
   - Extreme irritation over small things
   - Inability to unwind in the evenings
   - Waking regularly at night or early in the mornings
   - Difficulty in taking decisions
   - Inability to stop thinking about problems or the day's events
   - Tearfulness
   - Convictions that you just can't cope
   - Lack of enthusiasm even for cherished interests
   - Reluctance to meet new people and attempt new experiences
   - Inability to say 'no' when asked to do something
   - Having more responsibility than you can handle.

3. Are you *more* or *less* optimistic than you used to be (or about the same)?

4. Do you enjoy *watching* sport?

5. Can you get up late at weekends if you want to without feeling guilty?

6. Within reasonable professional and personal limits, can you speak your mind to: a) your boss? b) your colleagues? c) members of your family?

7. Who usually seems to be responsible for making the important decisions in your life: a) yourself? b) someone else?

8. When criticised by superiors at work, are you usually: a) very upset? b) moderately upset? c) mildly upset?

9. Do you finish the working day feeling satisfied with what you have achieved: a) often? b) sometimes? c) only occasionally?

10. Do you feel most of the time that you have unsettled conflicts with colleagues?

11. Does the amount of work you have to do exceed the amount of time available: a) habitually? b) sometimes? c) only very occasionally?

12. Have you a clear picture of what is expected of you professionally: a) mostly? b) sometimes? c) hardly ever?

13. Would you say that generally you have enough time to spend on yourself?

14. If you want to discuss your problems with someone, can you usually find a sympathetic ear?

15. Are you reasonably on course towards achieving your major objectives in life?

16. Are you bored at work: a) often? b) sometimes? c) very rarely?

17. Do you look forward to going into work: a) most days? b) some days? c) hardly ever?

18. Do you feel adequately *valued* for your abilities and commitment at work?

19. Do you feel adequately *rewarded* (in terms of status and promotion) for your abilities and commitment at work?

20. Do you feel your superiors: a) actively *hinder* you in your work? b) actively *help* you in your work?

21. If ten years ago you had been able to see yourself professionally as you are now, would you have seen yourself as: a) exceeding your expectations? b) fulfilling your expectations? c) falling short of your expectations?

22. If you had to rate how much you like yourself on a scale from 5 (most like) to 1 (least like), what would your rating be?

TURN TO PAGE 114 TO ASSESS YOUR RESULTS

general effects. There can be reasons for this not directly connected with stress, but in the great majority of cases, loss of your zest for life links with the increasing demands that same life is now making of you. Things that used to appeal to you now no longer hold attractions. The pressures upon you are gradually encroaching upon that space you used to have for yourself and for your hobbies and pastimes. What has happened is that life has become so earnest that any of your interests that don't carry a 'serious' label come to seem unimportant and time wasting. The only things that hold your attention are your work, and passive activities like watching television, which require nothing of you in the way of thinking or planning or judging (and which allow you to doze off and catch up on your sleep).

If you feel your zest for life has diminished, look again at the other effects in the three sections. It's likely that one or more of them will be apparent as well. In addition, look back at the physiological effects of stress given earlier in Chapter 1. Some of these things pass unnoticed, but effects upon the digestive system, upon heart rate, upon sex drive are obvious enough. Check these out, and see if a pattern emerges. The last thing I want to do is to encourage anyone to feel they're stressed if genuinely they're not. However, the insidious nature of many of the stressors to which we're subjected means that until we stop and take a long hard look at ourselves, we may ignore many of the warning signs until they begin to inflict more noticeable damage.

In addition to observing yourself for patterns of stress, it also pays to observe your friends and your colleagues. The more stressed they are, the more likely they are to pass some of their stress on to you. If stress is making them work less efficiently, or make faulty decisions, or displace their frustrations and aggressions upon others, you're bound to be affected. It will benefit you as well as them if you're able to recognise what's happening, not only because you may be able to give them some direct help with their problems, but because it will allow you to react less emotionally to them, thus saving some of the wear and tear upon your own nerves. The more we understand the strain other people are under and the effect that it is having upon them, the better we're able to be philosophical about their outbursts and shortcomings instead of taking them personally. It may also help us of course to stop adding our own twopennyworth to their problems. It's important to realise that we're not only the possible victims of stress, we're also potentially the stressors of other people. The unrealistic expectations, the unfair demands, the unnecessarily snappy answers that we hand out to others, may be the very things that they would put near the top of their lists if they're asked to say why *they* find life difficult. In organisations particularly, there's often a tendency to hand on the rebuke we've received from a superior to the person next in the hierarchy below us; or if we're in the caring professions, to be less sympathetic towards a client than we should be, or to be impatient with his or her helplessness instead of seeing it as just one of the symptoms that has made them into a client in the first place.

By stressing others, we make life more difficult for them. But in the long run, we also make it more difficult for ourselves. Subordinates become less loyal than they otherwise might be, less prepared to do more than the minimum, less eager to feed us with good ideas and creative strategies. Colleagues become less supportive, less ready to help us out, less ready to cover for us or listen to our problems. Clients become less co-operative, less appreciative, less ready to remember we're human as well. This is well illustrated by the teaching profession, where teachers who unnecessarily stress children find that their classes becomes less and less eager to learn, less and less rewarding to teach, and more and more inclined to produce those very problems of indiscipline and poor academic performance which the teacher's behaviour is supposedly designed to avoid in the first place.

I shall have more to say about these matters in later chapters when discussing stress avoidance strategies. But one doesn't have to be a sociologist or a social psychologist to realise that one over-stressed person in a work-team adds to the pressures upon everyone else. It isn't just that specific aspects of teamwork suffer: the actual environment within which that work takes place is impaired. Psychologists in the main seem a little coy about using the word 'happiness', primarily because of problems of definition. But we all recognise happiness in ourselves and in others when we see it, and we all recognise that a happy person enhances the lives of those in contact with him or her. One fraught stressed individual can bring a sense of strain to a whole office, and one sunny individual can lighten the atmosphere just as surely. So learning to handle stress in ourselves, and learning how not to stress others, is as valuable a contribution to the psychological health of a community as many much more widely advertised palliatives.

Chapter Three

What Causes Too Much Stress?

— the environment

STRESS MANAGEMENT

If we go back to our Zen story at the start of Chapter 1, we see a good example of a person in a stressful environment. Everything seems to be conspiring against him. First the tiger that chases him, then the cliff, then the tiger waiting down below, then the two mice gnawing through his life support system. Most of us can probably all too readily find equivalents in our own lives to the tigers and the cliff and the mice, but we differ from the man in the story in that we can usually do something about our stressors. We aren't quite at their mercy in the way that he was. We can make up our minds to take constructive action, and in making up our minds we are in fact taking the first step in stress management. This first step is usually called *mobilisation*, and is followed by two further steps called respectively *knowledge* and *action*. I'll take each in turn.

MOBILISATION

Mobilisation is the simple decision that *something* must be done. We can't go on as we are. One way of putting this decision is in the form of the catch phrase 'there must be a better way'. Sadly, many people fail to take this step, and without it there can't be any progress. Studies show that some 60 per cent of people who find their jobs stressful have no stress management programme of any kind. They fail to recognise that there *must* be a better way. This is partly because when under stress there's a feeling of inertia towards anything other than the immediate grind of getting through the day. We lack the energy to do anything about changing the nature of this grind. However, once we've taken the decision to mobilise we have an expressed commitment towards change, and from then on it becomes easier to build up some momentum.

KNOWLEDGE

Having mobilised, we need to understand what it is we're mobilising against. This is done by asking ourselves the questions 'What are my stressors?', 'What needs to be done about them?' and 'What is stopping me from doing it?'.

ACTION

The final stage is to take action. As we shall see in due course, sometimes the things that 'are stopping me from doing it' may be outside our control, or too strong for us, in which case we may have to ignore (or adapt to) the stressor rather than take action about it. But where this isn't the case, we decide on what action to take and whether this can be 'immediate' or 'future'.

Having taken the *mobilisation* step, let's move to the *knowledge* stage, and start by making a precise list of the things that are pressurising us. And here I have to stress the use of the word *precise*. In a stress-reduction programme, there's little help to be gained through generalising. It's no good writing down for example that your job is stressful. Your 'job' is simply the label that you use to describe your employment. Business executive, social worker, doctor, teacher or whatever. The label is only a label, and can no more be stressful than it can be rewarding. What is stressful is certain things *about* your job. And here again we need to be specific. Not just 'the boss', but the habit the boss has of calling you to the office and leaving you standing there for five minutes before deigning to look up from the desk and telling you why it is you're currently out of favour. Or his or her habit of asking for detailed information about something just when you have your coat on ready to leave at the end of the afternoon. Or his or her practice of barking at you down the telephone, or blaming you for his or her own mistakes, or giving you a disgraceful reference every time you apply for another job. Each of these items, ranging from minor irritations to major traumas, contributes to the tension the boss produces in you. And though you can't get rid of the boss (without putting yourself in court), you may very well be able to develop strategies for handling at

least some of the individual stressors that he or she delights in direct-
ing at you.

It isn't possible for me to suggest what each of these individual
stressors may be in all the tension-promoting areas of your life nor how
your final list will look. Variations from person to person are enormous. But if I look in turn at what these tension-promoting areas are,
and give suggestions under each one, this should help you to carry out
the more detailed task of identifying the things that apply in your own
case and entering them in your list.

This chapter will concentrate on your place of work, looking first at
general professional stressors, that is at the things that lie largely
outside your immediate job and the responsibilities it carries, but
which nevertheless significantly influence the way you tackle it.

GENERAL CAUSES OF STRESS AT WORK

ORGANISATIONAL PROBLEMS

Poor general organisation can mean that there are frustrating delays
before you can get decisions taken on crucial issues. Or it may be
unclear who within the hierarchy is responsible for these decisions.
Organisational procedures may generally be inefficient and time-wast-
ing. The organisation may be perpetually short of money, so that
equipment and facilities are lacking, and it rarely proves possible to
spend £5 now in order to save £20 next year.

INSUFFICIENT BACK-UP

Shortage of clerical staff or of people in key (though apparently non-
essential) posts may mean your having to carry out tasks below the
level of your training and competence, and which take time away from
the work you should be doing. Typing letters, taking telephone calls,
transporting or setting up equipment all come within this category. So
do delays while equipment is waiting to be repaired, or while supplies
fail to materialise. Though apparently trivial, irritations of this kind
have an important cumulative effect. Not only do they interfere with
working efficiency, they leave individuals with the feeling that their
professional skills are under-valued if superiors are happy to see them
fritter their time away on routine tasks unconnected with these skills.
Perhaps most important of all, single-minded individuals report that
the constant need to divert their minds away from the proper task in
hand in order to attend to ancillary activities builds up an extreme

sense of frustration and anger, much of which they are unable to vent upon those actually responsible for their predicament.

LONG OR UNSOCIABLE HOURS

Working these hours is tiring and stressful in itself. The body has a natural rhythm (know technically as a *circadian rhythm*) over the 24-hour period. There is a time to sleep and a time to work, a time at which our metabolism is at its peak and a time at which it is at its lowest point, a time at which we work most efficiently and think most clearly, and a time at which the mind and body want to rest and recuperate. In addition to these major peaks and troughs there are a number of minor ones spread over the 24 hours (some people feel at their brightest early and mid-morning, and early evening for example, others at midday and late afternoon and evening). Our circadian rhythms are in part set by nature, which intends us to work from sunrise to sunset and recuperate during the hours of darkness, and in part by society, which demands that we start and finish our day rather later than is natural.

Extreme attempts to tamper with our innate circadian rhythms (as for example in shift work) or abrupt fluctuations from day to day (as for example in business people, police and hospital staff, who have to cope with sudden crises at all hours) prompts both physiological and psychological stress. Studies with shift workers show clearly the toll this takes in terms of stress-related illness. Such studies – and others with jet-lagged business executives – show interestingly that it is less stressful to *retard* the circadian rhythm than to *advance* it. Thus going to bed later and getting up later is less stressful than having to rise earlier and retire earlier.

But in addition to tampering with the circadian rhythm, long or unsociable hours have two other major stress-promoting effects. Firstly, if these hours are unpredictable, they prevent the individual from ever feeling secure from the demands of the job. At any time, he or she may be called on to cancel a social engagement in order to work late, or may be contacted while relaxing at home in order to attend to urgent problems that have arisen. Secondly, late or unsociable hours may in themselves interfere with the development of the personal relationships and the leisure interests upon which relief from stress heavily depends.

POOR STATUS, PAY AND PROMOTION PROSPECTS

With most professional people, part of their identity becomes bound up with their job. This is such an important issue, that I shall be returning to it at greater length in the next chapter. But for the moment the point I want to make is that however vital and useful it may seem to us, if our job is poorly regarded by society in general (or by our superiors or our political masters, or anyone else who has power over us), it's difficult to stop this rubbing off on our own sense of who we are and of how significant we are. It isn't easy to have a genuine feeling of personal worth if other people seem to regard what we're doing as of minor importance, or as the sort of thing that anyone with minimal training and abilities could do.

It's a sad fact that in the Western world many of the people with the most responsible jobs in society (the caring professions are a good example, but the same often applies to those in the lower echelons in business and industry) are given the lowest rewards and made to operate in the most inadequate working conditions. Good pay and good working conditions are not only valuable in themselves (good pay helps avoid the stress of financial problems, while good working conditions promote efficiency), they act as tangible proof that people really do value us, instead of simply handing out ritual compliments when it suits their own purposes.

Good promotion prospects add further to this sense of being in a valued profession, but they also serve as long-term objectives. Without such objectives, many people feel the stress caused by a frustration of their ambitions. They become acutely aware of the passing of time, and of their own stagnation and, ultimately, hopelessness.

UNNECESSARY RITUALS AND PROCEDURES

Obvious amongst these is a proliferation of form filling and paperwork. Individuals feel they spend as much time writing reports and completing returns as they do on the actual job itself. To make matters worse, much of this paperwork may appear unnecessary to them, and may even simply be the creation of administrators anxious to justify their own employment and to enhance their status by asserting their power to interfere in the professional lives of others.

Equal frustrations arise from too many meetings. In many professional and business organisations, individuals complain bitterly about the proliferation of committees and working parties, all of which make deep inroads upon their time. They complain of superiors who have little else to do except to schedule (often at desperately short notice) meeting after meeting, and then to use these meetings as excuses for boosting their own egos. They also complain of the stress caused by the meetings themselves, when slipshod agendas and poor direction from the Chair allow people to waste time with irrelevancies or become locked into heated exchanges.

UNCERTAINTY AND INSECURITY

Some people thrive on uncertainty. The great majority don't. It figures high on the list of stressors for many people in business and professional life. Uncertainty takes from us some of the familiar landmarks by which we orientate ourselves and stabilise our sense of who we are. Not for nothing does uncertainty feature amongst the so-called brainwashing techniques used in fact and fiction to break down the individual's resistance to indoctrination.

At work, uncertainty may take the form of frequent changes of policy, so that individuals never know exactly where they stand. Planning ahead becomes difficult, and no sooner do people reconcile themselves to one set of procedures or one set of decisions, than they're required to change their thinking and reconcile themselves to something quite different. At its worst, uncertainty can take the form of not knowing whether one is going to keep one's job or not. First it looks as if one will be made redundant, then it doesn't, then it does, then it doesn't. Morale quickly crumbles under this kind of stress, as the individual painfully tries to adapt and re-adapt to each phase of the gloom–salvation–gloom cycle.

At a slightly less threatening level, uncertainty can take the form of doubts over whether one is going to be moved to another, less attractive post, or be put to work under someone who hitherto has been lower down in the hierarchy, or be passed over in the promotion stakes, or be transferred to a different office or be put to work in a different section. Too much routine and predictability can make a job monotonous, but most individuals need a generous minimum of these things if they are to feel secure. Even welcome changes that create intense excitement can raise stress levels, as the Holmes–Rahe scale of life event stress ratings on page 32 shows. When these changes are unwelcome, unpredictable, and subject to conflicting swings first in one direction then in another, the result is potentially devastating.

SPECIFIC CAUSES OF STRESS AT WORK

Let's turn from these general considerations to stressors that relate more specifically to the job you have to do. These are localised stressors, less a feature of the job as such than of the way in which the job is handled at your own particular level.

THE HOLMES–RAHE SOCIAL ADJUSTMENT SCALE

Any changes in the routines of our lives – even welcome ones – can be stressful, both in terms of the way in which we perceive them and in terms of the increased incidence of physical illness and death that occur during the following 12 months. The Holmes–Rahe Scale assigns values (based upon the sample being told that marriage represents 50 points) attributed by a sample of 394 individuals to the life events concerned.

Events	Scale of impact
Death of spouse	100
Divorce	75
Marital separation	65
Jail term	63
Death of close family member	63
Personal injury or illness	53
Marriage	50
Dismissal from work	47
Marital reconciliation	45
Retirement	45
Change in health of family member	44
Pregnancy	40
Sex difficulties	39
Gain of new family member	39
Business readjustment	39
Change in financial state	38
Death of close friend	37
Change to different line of work	36
Change in number of arguments with spouse	35
Major mortgage	31
Foreclosure of mortgage or loan	30
Change in responsibilities at work	29
Son or daughter leaving home	29
Trouble with in-laws	29
Outstanding personal achievement	28
Partner begins or stops work	26
Begin or end school	26
Change in living conditions	25
Revision of personal habits	24
Trouble with boss	23
Change in work hours or conditions	20
Change in residence	20
Change in schools	20
Change in recreation	19
Change in church activities	19
Change in social activities	18
Small mortgage or loan	17
Change in sleeping habits	16
Change in number of family get-togethers	15
Change in eating habits	15
Vacation	13
Christmas	12
Minor violations of the law	11

Don't attempt to add up a 'score' on this Scale. The values are there simply to show the *relative* impact of stressful events, and give some indication of the wide range of stressors in our lives. And the list is by no means complete. Most people can add items to it, many of them likely to carry high values.

UNCLEAR ROLE SPECIFICATIONS

It's surprising how often we aren't given a clear brief on what it is we're supposed to do, or on where our responsibilities end and those of the next person take over. One of the main problems of this lack of clarity is that often we get blamed for something that goes wrong when in fact we didn't think it lay within our province at all. Some colleagues are adept at shifting blame onto us in this way, leaving us with a strong sense of grievance and resentment (mixed sometimes with guilt too; *was* the particular incident our responsibility after all, *should* we perhaps have foreseen it and taken steps to avoid it happening?). Unclear job specifications leave us vulnerable. If we do nothing we're told we should have acted. If we show initiative and act we're accused of exceeding our responsibilities or of trying to undermine colleagues or steal their thunder. A classic case of the double-bind (that unpleasant situation where every course of action open to us is wrong) in operation. Unclear role specifications also make it hard to assign priorities to our various tasks and to allocate appropriate amounts of time to each of them, two factors which are major sources of stress.

ROLE CONFLICT

Role-induced stress can also occur when two aspects of our job are incompatible with each other. In the case of the schoolteacher, the role of counsellor and helper to children in trouble can prove incompatible with the role of disciplinarian and upholder of school authority. In the case of the social worker, loyalty to a client may conflict with one's legal responsibilities. In the case of the nurse, good patient care may conflict with the tight routines and schedules which it is one's duty to observe. In the case of the manager, company loyalty may conflict with loyalty to subordinates or to clients.

Role conflict can furnish another instance of the double-bind: whatever one does is in the eyes of one set of criteria going to be wrong. This results in feelings of inner conflict, of threat of discovery and censure by superiors, and ultimately of inadequacy and poor self-image.

UNREALISTICALLY HIGH SELF-EXPECTATIONS (PERFECTIONISM)

Studies with teachers in particular have shown that unrealistically high self-expectations are one of the major causes of excessive stress. If we constantly expect too much of ourselves, we will drive ourselves too hard yet will forever be disappointed with the results. Unrealistic self-expectations are often linked to the unclear role specifications and the role conflicts mentioned above. Because it isn't clear what is expected of him or her, or because one aspect of the job is constantly clashing with another, the individual gets trapped in feelings of what 'ought' to be done. 'I *ought* to be covering that area as well as this.' 'I *ought* to be able to function effectively both in this aspect of my role and in that.' 'I *ought* to be able to be fair both to person A and person B.'

The result of such lack of realism is that the individual is never satisfied with his or her performance and can never relax with the feeling of a job well done. By failing to recognise the limitations and the constraints within which we all have to work, individuals are prevented from developing accurate criteria by which to measure the success or otherwise of their efforts, and ultimately prevented from performing as well as they otherwise might. (This links with over-conscientiousness, discussed in Chapter 5.)

A further consequence is a reluctance to *delegate*: 'Because others won't do the job as well (or in the same way!) as me, I end up trying to do everything myself, instead of accepting other people's ideas may be as good as my own and that in any case the ability to delegate is an essential quality in the good manager.'

INABILITY TO INFLUENCE DECISION MAKING (POWERLESSNESS)

In certain circumstances (for instance when ill or when faced with an emergency) studies show that some people find it less stressful if they have no powers of decision. They find it more soothing to leave things in the hands of the experts, and not have to agonise over which choice to make. Even in less challenging situations indecisive and highly insecure individuals may prefer to have inflexible superiors or protocols governing their lives, thus removing any need for self-determination.

But for most of the time and for most people, a degree of say in one's own life lowers the levels of potential stress. At work, most individuals like to feel that they have some power to influence events, and that their personal preferences and their ideas for improving job efficiency are going to receive a hearing. The feeling of powerlessness is not only detrimental to our sense of status and personal worth, it produces high levels of frustration when we can recognise shortcomings in the present system and identify a better way of doing things, yet find ourselves ignored or worse still shouted down.

FREQUENT CLASHES WITH SUPERIORS

Poor relationships with our superiors are a potent source of stress since these superiors have the ability to influence our lives materially. They can manipulate our duties and our working conditions, give or withold promotion, increase or lower our status in the eyes of our peers, and offer or refuse the favourable reference that will have a crucial effect on our chances of successfully applying for other jobs. Small wonder that an unsympathetic boss can dominate so much of our professional lives.

Another stressor in worker–boss relationships is the boss who consistently fails to give credit where we feel it has been earned. This leaves us with the feeling that we are under-valued, and can blunt both our enjoyment of the job and our incentive to enhance our performance and strive for further advancement. Yet another source of stress is the boss who constantly niggles and criticises, or the boss who is unable to delegate, habitually interferes in what we are doing, and never allows us the freedom to take our own decisions. Such a boss frustrates our creativity and enthusiasm, makes us doubt our own competence at times, forces us into an adult–child stereotype, and gives us the feeling that we're never free from hostile scrutiny.

ISOLATION FROM COLLEAGUES' SUPPORT

This is a particular problem in occupations (such as teaching, social work, the police force) where we spend most of our time with clients and very little in the company of colleagues. Opportunities to discuss our professional problems, to obtain sympathy and reassurance, and to comfort ourselves with the knowledge that colleagues are experiencing similar difficulties to our own, are severely limited, and in addition we're often denied the feedback that comes from peer group comment and appraisal. We vary in the extent of our self-sufficiency. Some individuals rate isolation from colleagues as a positive advantage, but for the majority, it leads to increased feelings of vulnerability and to depleted professional resources.

Many people claim that isolation also causes additional pressures within the job itself. It means that no one else is properly familiar with the details of our case load or of the particular professional tasks we're undertaking. This makes it much harder for us to take leave, to be off sick, or to attend training or refresher courses, If no one else can step adequately into our shoes at short notice we feel that through our absence we are both failing our clients and burdening our colleagues.

OVERWORK AND TIME PRESSURES

Few human beings perform at their best when under constant pressures. In addition to holidays and formal breaks each day such as lunch and mid-morning coffee, we need short intervals between finishing one demanding task and turning to the next: time to draw breath, to look around us, to relax the mind with a little day-dreaming, to re-orientate our thinking before plunging back into the fray. We also need those occasional slack days when we've actually cleared our in-trays and can potter about a little, reorganising our filing system, looking through catalogues for ideas on new pieces of equipment to order if the cash squeeze ever lifts. Such momentary respites are of inestimable value in resisting stress. Without them, we feel hounded and trapped, with never a moment to ourselves or a moment in which to stand still and look objectively at our job and the way in which we're trying to handle it.

We also need respite from constant battles to meet deadlines. I mentioned in Chapter 1 that sometimes we need the incentive of working to pressures and to fixed schedules, but very few of us need this to happen all the time. I instanced Balzac's prodigious literary output when his creditors threatened, but it's highly unlikely that Balzac could have produced any great novels if he'd had to work like this all the time. In the intervals when he'd paid off his debts, he stopped writing and went on extravagant spending sprees. I'm not advocating the life style of a Balzac, but he does demonstrate for us the need for those moments when we can experience freedom from our work, however much we may enjoy it.

LACK OF VARIETY

Freedom is also achieved through a measure of variety within the framework of what we're doing. The human mind requires the stimuli of fresh experiences from time to time if it is to stay concentrated and creative. Many professional posts carry this variety for at least part of the time. No two clients, no two patients, no two schoolchildren, no two emergencies are ever quite the same. But in particular the administrative duties attached to these posts can involve monotony. Some professionals confess to near panic when travelling to work if they know that each morning's events are going to follow the same pattern. At 9.30 the post will arrive and have to be dealt with. At 10.00 the boss will summon everyone into his or her office for morning briefing. At 10.30 the trolley will arrive with morning tea or coffee. It isn't that any of these things in themselves is unwelcome, it's simply that predictability had moved beyond the point at which it is reassuring to become drab and constricting.

Trying to rationalise their panic, people tend to say that the uniformity of certain aspects of their job reminds them acutely of the passing of time. They see themselves doing the same things at the same time next year and the year after and for the foreseeable years to come. The only difference is that each year they themselves will be a little older and a little greyer. 'And yet', they add in some perplexity, 'I do *like* my job really; it's just that. . . .'

POOR COMMUNICATION

However well people work together as individuals, poor channels of communication are often reported as a potent source of stress. No one seems clear who should be told what, nor when he or she needs to be told it. No one seems clear how to get hold of person X or person Y at short notice, nor how to check that person A or person B has received a copy of the vital memo they've just been sent (the odds are they'll swear they haven't). To make matters worse, no one seems sure how to obtain the information they need from colleagues before they commit themselves to action. Someone has the information somewhere, and would be only too ready to share it, but no one is sure who that someone is.

The usual consequences of poor channels of communication are that people take decisions without being in possession of accurate facts, are unable to pass on important details to the relevant quarters, attend meetings inadequately briefed, and are generally left with feelings of reduced control over events. The guilty party behind all this may be an administrator who is not doing his or her job properly, or someone higher up the hierarchy who has not created a proper communications system, or an inadequate internal post or telephone network, or the tendency of the job itself to disperse people to inaccessible places. But it can turn a straightforward attempt to give or receive information from a brief, low-stress task into a lengthy (and often ultimately fruitless) high-stress one.

INADEQUATE LEADERSHIP

People vary in the extent to which they want strong leadership. And leaders of course vary in their styles from authoritarian to democratic to laissez-faire. But weak or inadequate leadership, or a leadership style which is unsuited to the needs of people lower down the hierarchy, create a power vacuum. Once you have a power vacuum, unpleasant things are apt to fill it. Like power struggles between colleagues nominally at the same level. Or like attempts to bring pressure upon the leadership to side with one faction or with another. While the power vacuum lasts, it may also be impossible to get crucial decisions taken, or to get leadership support when conflicts develop with outside parties. Since a leader also has a *training* function, there may be inadequate guidance given to new members of staff. And since a leader also has a *restraining* function, there may be inadequate attempts to curb undesirable initiatives on the part of some established members of staff, or to curb the inappropriate use of power by more senior individuals.

CONFLICTS WITH COLLEAGUES

Partly as a result of inadequate leadership, partly as a result of personality clashes, and partly as a result of many of the other variables discussed above, such as unclear role specifications and overwork, fertile opportunities for clashes between colleagues exist in most organisations. The fight for status, or to defend territory or 'privileges' add further opportunities, and all too often the day becomes a succession of bruising encounters between individuals who all have so much to gain from working in harmony. In an atmosphere thick with accusations and counter-accusations, with denials and counter-denials, few people can really give of their best or think well of others and ultimately of themselves.

INABILITY TO FINISH A JOB

This may be due to a number of factors, such as time pressures, poor general organisation at higher levels, or poor communication. But much job satisfaction comes from seeing a finished product at the end of one's labours. Constantly being switched from one task to another before any of them is properly finished greatly reduces this satisfaction, and leads to feelings of frustration and bitterness. It also interferes with the professional relationships that you may be building with clients, and equally importantly interferes with the learning process. If you're rarely able to see a job right through, you cannot assess the value of the various strategies you employed during the course of it, and are therefore unable to use this information to improve your future performance.

FIGHTING UNNECESSARY BATTLES

Again this is often the combined result of many of the factors discussed in this section. Few things waste energy and enthusiasm more surely than the constant need to fight battles which with better planning and greater task-awareness by superiors could easily have been avoided. The individual feels not only that he or she has to face the legitimate struggles associated with the job, but a host of illegitimate ones as well.

TASK-RELATED CAUSES OF STRESS AT WORK

In addition to general and specific stressors related to a job itself, there are also stressors that arise from the day-to-day tasks contained within a job. These are stressors related actually to doing the job, as opposed to stressors related to the conditions under which you're expected to do it. They vary a great deal from job to job and even from hour to hour, but there are a number that are consistently reported by people analysing their own experiences.

DIFFICULT CLIENTS OR SUBORDINATES

This one speaks for itself. In all branches of business and professions involving close work with people, there's scope for friction and conflict. Individuals report that clashes with clients hurt them most when they are either *totally unexpected*, or *unfair and unjustified*. In the first instance, there isn't time to muster defences. You anticipate a neutral or even a pleasant meeting, and are faced instead with hostility and verbal aggression. In the second instance, you face accusations and blame which belong properly to the system rather than to individuals forced to work within it. Or you catch the brunt of misunderstandings or of misplaced antagonisms. The feeling of hurt is made worse when you're genuinely doing your best to help your client, and when you might reasonably look for credit and appreciation.

Some individuals confess actually to enjoy conflict with clients or subordinates. They find it stimulates them and keeps them on their toes. But in the great majority of cases it imposes unhappy feelings which can persist for days and even weeks after the event. You replay the incident repeatedly in your imagination, sometimes handling it differently, sometimes trying to stay calmer, but always with the same nasty aftertaste. Often people confess that things aren't helped by the need to stay 'polite' and 'professional' during the actual encounter itself. They can't have their say and release their real feelings. Others acknowledge that on the occasions when they *have* lost their control and shouted back, they've felt much worse about it afterwards, and seen it as a poor reflection upon their competence at the job. This 'no-win' aspect of dealing with difficult clients or subordinates substantially increases the stress factor.

INSUFFICIENT TRAINING

As the demands and the complexities of most executive and professional jobs increase inexorably, it isn't surprising that people within these jobs find themselves short of the professional skills needed to cope. They feel they have had insufficient training for many of the tasks which they're called upon to do, and when they look closer they often feel that such training isn't possible anyway. The pace of change is so great in modern times that the development of new training methods to cope with all eventualities just can't keep pace.

An additional stressor is that the amount of knowledge required just to stay in one place is reaching staggering proportions in most professions. In medicine for example, in scientific and technical walks of life, as well as in teaching, the rate at which new ideas, techniques and research findings are coming onto the market is growing exponentially. The struggle to absorb them all, to keep up to date, to be armed with the right answers, takes more and more time and energy each year. Once again, the double-bind can operate. Either you wear yourself out trying to cope with the unequal task, or you allow yourself to fall behind and are left with negative feelings about your level of commitment and professional expertise.

EMOTIONAL INVOLVEMENT WITH CLIENTS OR SUBORDINATES

You don't magically leave personal feelings behind when you qualify as a social worker or nurse or doctor or teacher, or when you take on managerial responsibilities. You don't discard feelings of like and dislike for example, of sympathy and antipathy, of love even and hate. Many of those in professional life suggest that these human emotions can cause them more stress at times than almost anything else. Nurses and doctors have to watch patients to whom they have become deeply attached die. Social workers have to make agonising decisions which involve splitting up families, or have to struggle to feel sympathetic towards clients who do their best to forfeit all sympathy. Teachers have to try to behave impartially towards all their children. Managers have to take decisions affecting the careers of others. And all professionals often have to cope with the intense feelings of clients or subordinates who have become attached to *them*, either dependently or romantically.

It's all too easy to say that no good professional allows his or her personal feelings to enter into things. Life doesn't work like that. When dealing with one's own and other people's emotions, life frequently becomes confused and messy. I shall return to this issue when dealing with the more personal aspects of stress in due course, but since our present purpose is to identify professional stressors, it's important to face up to the existence of feelings towards clients, and to identify the circumstances which seem most to give rise to them. In what situations are these feelings most likely to occur? In what (and towards what) kind of client? What does one do to invite or encourage these feelings? What signals does one give to clients? How does one handle these feelings, both in oneself and in one's client, during the early stages when they can best be dealt with? By clarifying the position in this way, one is in a better position to develop strategies for handling it in the future.

THE RESPONSIBILITIES OF THE JOB

By the nature of their tasks, many people in the caring professions and in executive and managerial positions are called upon almost daily to make decisions vitally affecting the health and well-being of other (often highly vulnerable) people. In some cases, they may also be making crucial financial decisions, which have far-reaching consequences for their organisation and for the people who work within it or who are dependent upon it. Though some professionals talk about developing a 'thick skin' over a period of time, and thus seeing their decision making as simply part of their job, others condemn this approach as leading to insensitivity and ultimately to decisions which fail to take full account of the human factor. To the busy doctor, social worker, manager, teacher or police officer each individual may simply be another in the long list of clients or subordinates or members of the public with whom they have to deal. But to the individual concerned, he or she is of course a unique person, with a special problem that needs attention. In some cases, this may be the only time they have ever asked for professional help. To see them as just another statistic in the case book is to ignore their humanity and ignore the real nature of what they may currently be going through as well as the real consequences that your decisions may have for them.

Taking each client or subordinate as an individual does, however, impose its own kind of strain upon the professional concerned. You have to come to each client's problem with the same freshness, the same concern that he or she brings to it. This is one of the major factors that counsellors and social workers list when they're discussing the phenomenon of 'burn-out', that stage when they seem no longer able to concentrate upon clients' problems, to provide the necessary support, to think clearly in their responses. We seem to have a finite store of energy, and when it's used up we need a period away from the job before it can be replenished.

Social workers, teachers, medical personnel and police officers are all prominent amongst the professional groups who report that stress factors in their work are now greatly increased by the degree of public scrutiny which is currently brought to bear upon them. Their successes for the most part go unacknowledged, but their every mistake is picked upon by the media and by various public bodies. While not denying the necessity (in fact desirability) of public scrutiny, the professional groups involved argue that when it goes beyond a certain point, it actually inhibits them from taking the decisions which it is their responsibility to take. They become over-cautious, prone to see inaction as the lesser of two evils, or conversely to see *any* decision, however inappropriate, as being better than facing the accusation of having done nothing at all.

INABILITY TO HELP OR ACT EFFECTIVELY

All professional people like to feel they have the skills needed to solve the problems which face them in their work. Doctors and nurses want to heal, counsellors want to help people change, teachers want to teach, managers want to manage and so on. Where we call on all our skills, and yet fail to produce the desired effect, there is a feeling of impotence, of professional fallibility, and also what some people describe as resentment towards the patient or the client or the schoolchild. With so much being done for them, they jolly well *ought* to get better/re-shape their lives/learn and pass exams/increase production or sales figures. Though it's recognised that this feeling is often irrational, and bears no relation to the real condition of the patient/client/schoolchild/work force, it's nevertheless difficult to control, and sometimes leads to a temptation to wash our hands altogether of the individuals concerned, and feel they've brought this dismissal upon themselves by their stubborn refusal to co-operate.

The inability to help can also lead, particularly in those with a very strong sense of vocation, to feelings of failure at the personal level. Another human being has turned to you, with trust and confidence, for help, and you haven't been able to provide it. In some people, this leads to questions about their suitability for the profession. A good healer ought to be able to heal, a good teacher ought to be able to teach, a good manager ought to be able to manage. If we can't do these things, then perhaps we ought to go and find some other sort of work which we can do more effectively. Doubts of this kind about one's professional suitability are more common in younger professionals than in those with more experience, and often have to do with an unrealistic level of professional expectation. But they're common enough in all age groups, and lead to genuine soul-searching and distress.

STRESS IN THE HOME

Many of the items in the Holmes–Rahe Social Adjustment Scale on page 32 are related to events outside work, and generally studies show that in many cases domestic stress rivals stress at work in making people's lives difficult. So although the focus of this book is upon stress at work, we can't ignore domestic stress. Not only because in many cases it rivals stress at work in pressurising people, but because a *non-stressful* and supportive life within the home is a powerful aid to coping with stress outside it.

Studies show that the main sources of stress in and around the home can be summarised under the following headings:

1. Stress caused by a partner

2. Stress caused by children

3. Stress caused by domestic arrangements

4. Stress caused by environmental pressures upon the home

Both partner-induced and children-induced stress arise mainly as a result of clashes either of temperament or of interests (though illness or disability in partner or children can also play a part). Stress caused by domestic arrangements – which can often be linked to partner and children stress – is usually a consequence of having too many household duties and too little time in which to do them. Environmental stress comes from such diverse sources as noisy neighbours, road or building works that threaten the value or enjoyment of one's property, and financial worries brought on by the inability to pay household bills.

As with stress at work, an essential step in dealing with domestic stress is to make a cool and accurate appraisal of where the stress comes from. Be frank about it. Sometimes it's disturbing to admit even to yourself that a much-loved partner or child is, however unwittingly, making your life difficult. But unless the admission is made, there isn't much you can do to put things right.

HOW TO USE YOUR LIST

Once you've made out your list of professional stressors, using these or similar headings, the next step is to see what can be done to eliminate or reduce any of them. We'll look at how to go about this in the next chapter.

Chapter Four

Managing Your Environment

Peter: a case study of how to manage environmental causes of stress

❑ Let's look at how Peter, a 33-year-old qualified social worker,
tackled the task of dealing with environmental stressors. Peter
is married with two children aged six and four. His wife is also
a qualified social worker, but since returning to employment
after the younger child started nursery school she has chosen to
work part time in a bookshop. Her earnings make only a small
contribution to the family budget, but she is able to take
responsibility for ferrying the children to and from school each
day. Peter confesses to finding his job very stressful, and has
begun to doubt whether he wishes to continue it much longer.
He talks rather vaguely of opening a bookshop with his wife 'as
soon as she's had a bit more experience of how to run things'.

When asked to make a list of his work-related stressors, Peter
doubted at first whether this was possible. He argued that the
stress of his job was so general and all-pervasive that he
couldn't really isolate individual things. However he agreed to
try, and quickly became enthusiastic about the task. He found
that if he thought hard enough about it, he was able to see that
his job wasn't one big stressor after all, but a collection of small
stressors, some of relatively minor importance in themselves,
but which added together represented a formidable amount of
pressure. After completing his list, he said he felt better about
his stress already. Breaking things down into individual stress
components helped him to see things as more manageable, and

to feel in consequence more positive and optimistic about his ability to cope.

Peter's list went like this, with additional comments as shown.

Poor back-up   'In my job, there are often umpteen phone calls for you when you're out of the office. We do have someone to take the calls, but she has other jobs as well, and isn't always there. And frequently people say they've rung in and left me an important message, but I don't get it and nobody seems to know anything about it. What irritates me most is the people who ring in and simply leave a number for me to call back. Often they only want routine things, and I waste hours trying to contact them. There's also a delay in getting letters typed. They're supposed to be checked and corrected before I get them for signature, but I still usually find mistakes, which wastes more time while they go back to be done again.'

Too many meetings   'I seem to work for people who are only happy when they're calling meetings. Even some of the case-conferences we have could be shortened or avoided altogether if we had a more workable system for circulating information to people and getting their comments. Some people seem to think that as long as they're in a meeting they're working. I just sit there and think of all the other things I could usefully be doing.'

Uncertainty   'We're going through a period of constant change and reorganisation. Rumours keep coming around about people being moved to other jobs. No one seems to know whether they're true or not, and until they're contradicted everyone gets in a flap and feels suspicious of everyone else. You never really know what to believe, or who your friends are.'

Unclear role   'I accept I'm not in the sort of job where you can lay down precisely what people are supposed to do and not to do. A lot depends upon your own conscience anyway. But I get really wound up when I'm told *after* the event that something was my responsibility, and that it's my fault things have gone wrong. It's just someone else passing the buck, either a more experienced colleague or my boss. I also hate it when I've done a good piece of work and someone else steps in and takes the credit. That happens quite often, and if you make a fuss about it people go around saying you're being childish, and that it's the job that counts and not the pats on the back. My unclear role also makes it hard for me to assess and arrange my priorities. I'm often at a loss to know which are the vital jobs and which are the ones that can wait.'

Poor pay 'I suppose the pay isn't that bad, though with a young family and my wife only in a part-time job, we always seem to be hard up. But it irks me when I see people in other jobs and without half my responsibility earning more than I do. I've a friend who's a solicitor and another who's an estate agent, and they can easily earn three times as much from a day's work as I do. And it doesn't seem to me they're really being much use to anyone.'

Powerlessness 'Decisions are taken above my head a lot of the time, and by people who really know nothing about the kind of work I have to do. I don't feel I have anywhere near enough say in my own professional life. I've tried to complain, but I'm listened to either with impatience or with so much condescension I feel like a small kid again.'

Poor communications 'If we ever did have a system, it's broken down. I suppose in a way this comes back to insufficient back-up. If we had proper clerical help, and someone who had the time to sit down and devise a proper system for making sure that the right information gets to the right people at the right time, it would take off a lot of the pressure. I seem to spend half my life going around pretending I know things when I don't, and pretending I've been told when I haven't. The trouble is I always end up thinking it's *my* fault if I'm not properly in the picture, and that stops me from being more open about it.'

Overwork 'I ought to enjoy it when I'm given a new case to work on, because that's my job and that's why I came into social work. But these days my heart usually sinks. I know how difficult it's going to be to tackle the case properly. I feel trapped. I'm sick of having to fudge things. I know it's the fault of the system and not of me, but I'm beginning to feel I'm just not much good at what I do. And although I don't really mind the responsibility of being involved in big decisions about people's lives, I hate having to do it when I know I haven't been able to spend enough time on a case to get to know it properly.'

Peter added in a number of smaller stressors, but he was convinced that these were the major ones. When asked to place them in rank order, from the most to the least stressful, he produced this list:

1. *Overwork*

2. *Unclear role*

3. *Powerlessness*

4. *Poor back-up*

5. *Too many meetings*

6. *Poor communications*

7. *Poor pay*

8. *Uncertainty*

Peter's list may differ, of course, in content and in rank order from those produced by other social workers, and by people in other professions, since stress is very much a personal and situational thing.

Sandra: a case study of how to manage environmental causes of stress

❏ For example Sandra, a final-year student nurse, also put overwork at the head of her list, and echoed what Peter had to say about overwork leaving her feeling inadequate at her job. But next to overwork she put poor pay ('Not just for me but because it stops people from staying in the profession and coming into it in the first place') and followed this with organisational problems ('Working conditions are bad and getting worse; we always seem short of things') and unsociable hours. Her full list went like this:

1. *Overwork*

2. *Poor Pay*

3. *Unsociable hours*

4. *Inability to finish a job*

5. *Unrealistically high self-expectations*

6. *Unnecessary working rituals*

Discussing her list, she wondered whether she had placed 'inability to finish a job' too low down. With her growing experience and her growing understanding of medical conditions and patient needs, she felt an essential part of her job was talking to patients, reassuring them, making them feel comfortable, giving them details about their treatment. But because of staff shortages 'and the inability of the powers-that-be to recognise how much of a nurse's job this really is', she usually found herself called away whenever she tried to spend time with a patient. She was even made sometimes to feel that by talking to patients she was shirking other jobs. The worst experiences of her hospital life, she emphasised, was when someone died and she felt she hadn't even had time to get to know them, to listen to them, and to share something of their last days with them.

Like Peter and like many other people in the caring professions, Sandra also spoke frequently of times when she blamed herself for not being better at her job. But in her case, she recognised that much of this came from setting herself too high standards. She had an ideal of what a good nurse should be like, and never felt she was quite able to match up to it. Partly she felt this resulted from a system which had given her too much responsibility too soon, and which hadn't allowed her sufficient time to watch experienced nurses going about their jobs and thus build a reasonable picture of what was and what wasn't possible.

But the only time Sandra became really resentful was when she talked about the unnecessary working rituals that she found in the profession. She understood that things were much better than they used to be, but she still felt that though on the one hand she had too much responsibility, on the other she was often treated like a child by her superiors, and not allowed to have a proper say in working routines and practices. Equally, she felt irritated by what she called the 'pecking order' in her hospital, stretching from consultants at the top down to cleaners at the bottom. She was convinced that the vast differences in salary and status were unfair, and didn't reflect the actual jobs that people did and the day-to-day responsibilities they undertook. Sometimes she felt so put-down by the people above her in the pecking order that she 'seethed about it' for a long time afterwards, and ended up snapping at her patients.

DEALING WITH CAUSES OF STRESS

Many people feel, like Peter, that the very act of identifying the precise stressors that make life difficult is helpful. It seems to make the problem more tangible. But of course, the exercise doesn't end there. The real object is to do something about these stressors. Each one must be tabbed in one of three ways: 'immediate action', 'future action', or 'ignore or adapt to'. 'Immediate action' covers those stressors about which something can be done now, today or within the next few days. 'Future action' covers those about which action can be taken, but it isn't yet clear what, or if it is clear, nothing can be done until a more appropriate time. 'Ignore or adapt to' covers those stressors which are beyond reach at least for the forseeable future, and which just have to be coped with as they are.

I shall return to the subject of 'Ignore' stressors in Chapter 6, which leaves the other two categories to be dealt with now. Let's look at Peter's list and see how he tabbed it.

1. *Overwork* – future action

2. *Unclear role* – immediate action

3. *Powerlessness* – ignore or adapt to

4. *Poor back-up* – ignore or adapt to

5. *Too many meetings* – future action

6. *Poor communications* – immediate action

7. *Poor pay* – ignore or adapt to

8. *Uncertainty* – immediate action

Peter arrived at these tabs by deciding sensibly not to add to his stressors by fighting battles he couldn't win. There was no chance of his winning more power for himself without a major change in the system, while the chances of more back-up were remote unless and until more money was made available by the politicians. Overwork was a major issue, and although he could identify the main cause behind it (too heavy a case load) he knew it would take time to decide what could best be done about it. So he put it on the back burner for the moment, while he concentrated on other issues.

PETER'S IMMEDIATE ACTION

UNCLEAR ROLE

Peter started with this one because it was near the top of his list and because in some ways it was the easiest to deal with. (In a dauntingly long list, tackle the easy ones first, to give yourself the scent of success, rather than go straight for the very big issues.) When he applied for his job, he'd been sent a job description. But he'd soon found it too inaccurate and too vague to be of any use. So now, drawing upon his actual experience of what the job entailed, he made a careful breakdown of each area of his job, listing precisely the priorities in that area, and what he might reasonably be expected to do in order to cope effectively with them. He then made a separate list of the things which he often found himself doing, but which really didn't form part of the job as he understood it.

Peter describes himself as fortunate in being on quite good terms with his chief and in knowing that the latter rather prides herself on being open to new ideas. He thus felt able to go to his chief directly with his role specifications. If he hadn't been on good terms with the chief, he says he would have gone to his colleagues first, and interested them in the idea of putting together role specifications which could form the basis for a united approach. 'Being something of a psychologist', Peter was careful to use the buzz term 'role negotiation' when he requested an interview with the chief. During the interview, he explained that the job was becoming so complex and changing so rapidly that it was increasingly difficult for anyone to know precisely what it was they were supposed to cover. He was careful not to look as if he was apportioning blame, and was careful to protect his superior's self-esteem by referring to her stated wish that staff should always think creatively about what it was they were supposed to be doing. The core of his argument was that staff should be asked to 'negotiate' their roles with the chief, so that everyone could be sure what was expected of whom.

The chief liked Peter's approach, and without commitment invited each of Peter's colleagues to submit a similar set of job specifications. Rather to her surprise (and to her admitted relief) she found that most people assigned rather more duties to themselves than she herself would have done. In consultation with everyone, she then formalised these specifications, so that everyone knew what was expected of them, and agreed to review and amend them regularly. She was also prepared to look closely at the things which people up to now had found themselves doing but which were really outside their remit, and to take steps to see that they were as far as possible protected from these demands in future.

POOR COMMUNICATIONS

Peter decided to be bold about this one, and to make a record of all the pieces of information that should have reached him but had failed to do so over the last weeks. He was surprised at how long the list was, even though he was sure it wasn't fully complete. He then identified existing channels and procedures which should have ensured that all the missing information reached him. With the approval of his chief, he circulated a detailed breakdown of these channels and procedures to his colleagues, and invited suggestions for their improvement at certain key points. The upshot was that the communications network was properly formalised for the first time, with everyone clear on how they fitted into it. Some weeks later Peter reported that although the network still isn't functioning perfectly, everyone seems happy that it's greatly improved and suggestions for making it better still are readily forthcoming.

UNCERTAINTY

Peter decided to tackle this one humorously, since he was well aware how important laughter can be in reducing stress. Together with a colleague who Peter says is much better at these things than he is himself, he has started a monthly broadsheet called *Rumour Record*. Illustrated with jokey cartoons, this is pinned on the noticeboard and contributions are invited from anyone who's heard a good rumour. Peter has promised a small prize to the 'rumour hunter of the month', and says he's delighted by the response he's had from everyone. Not only are people now better able to laugh at rumours, they're also actively looking for them, which Peter says has in a strange way begun to alter people's attitudes towards them. Something of the fear of rumours has gone, to be replaced by the collector's zeal. He isn't sure, but he also has the feeling that people higher up in the hierarchy are now much quicker to scotch rumours in which they're implicated than they used to be, and that generally there's less uncertainty in the air.

OVERWORK

Tabbing this for future action has meant that Peter is giving himself time to examine the problem in some detail. He says that clearer role specification and improved communications have both eased something of the burden upon him, but he is now identifying the precise aspects of his job that are causing him to work too hard, to see if it is possible to rationalise and reorganise any of them. He has a feeling, now that this exercise is underway, that he hasn't been using his time very efficiently. He sees no chance of reducing his case load, but he says he's surprised by the number of wasted journeys he makes every week through lack of forward planning, and by his rather disorganised itineraries, which often result in his covering many more miles in the course of the day than he actually need. He also says that he's working on a more structured approach to the time he spends interviewing clients, so that he can get the information he needs or give the necessary help more quickly and effectively. He's identified that he finds it hard to come to the point with certain clients, and hard to get away from others. There are clear strategies for doing these things (see page 54), and he is resolved to practise them more effectively in future. He realises that although it's important to make good social contact with clients, too much time is currently being frittered away discussing – or listening to – irrelevancies.

SANDRA'S ACTION

Sandra had more problems with her list of stressors. She felt on studying it that there was very little she could do about any of the items. This brought her to the conclusion that she would either have to develop 'ignore' skills, or decide that ultimately nursing was too stressful for her, and that she would be best advised to start thinking about other work. She felt it important not to see a decision to leave the profession as a sign of failure, but as a courageous and positive move, dictated by realism and a perfectly proper concern for her own welfare and career satisfaction.

At the moment, Sandra is working on her 'ignore' skills, and is still in nursing 'at least till I finish my training'. She has however had another think about her list, and has decided that there are after all certain actions she can take. She has come to the conclusion that nurses are

HOW TO STRUCTURE INTERVIEWS

Some clients have a need to talk, perhaps because of loneliness, perhaps because of an over-preoccupation with themselves, perhaps because they have something to say. But a professional only has so much time to devote to each client. When time is short, or when it's clear that the interview is serving no useful purpose for either party, it's vital to know how to terminate it efficiently and without giving offence.

This is difficult if you are with a client who (deliberately or unwittingly) is insensitive to the polite social signals we normally give when we want to break off a conversation (e.g. glancing at the clock, 'Well I must be off', 'Okay I'll be in touch', getting to one's feet, reaching for hat or gloves). In such cases, there are clear procedures that facilitate matters.

Make it clear during the greeting phase of the interview that you have to be away by a certain time ('I can only stay until 10 past', 'I shall have to be off sharp at 10 to').

During the interview, keep the client focused on the relevant topics. If he or she wanders off, guide them back by asking for help (e.g. 'That's interesting, but I still need help in clarifying what you were telling me a moment ago', 'I still haven't grasped the point about . . .', 'I'm not clear on your answer to my question'.

Give your information briskly and briefly. Be decisive. Don't hesitate. Rehearse much of what you're going to say *before* the interview

If the client has the habit of interrupting you whenever you're trying to say something, just keep talking, calmly and confidently, until you've finished. Don't raise your voice to compete. Act as if you're the only one talking. It will mean you are both talking at once initially, but he or she will soon get the message.

Get to your feet promptly at the stated time; act decisively and say the conventional words of parting *after* you've crossed the threshold out of the house or room. If the interview is on your own territory, hold the door open for your client to depart. Use forms of words that reassure your client that you'll be meeting again soon, but that for now the interview is over (e.g. 'I look forward to seeing you next week, but you must excuse me now as someone else is waiting').

powerless in matters like pay, conditions and status largely through choice. Patients' lives are just as dependent upon good nursing care as they are upon the skills of the consultant, and the reason nurses as a body don't enjoy anything like the same kind of benefits is that they haven't taken a conscious decision to assert themselves. Sandra says that many of her colleagues just accept their lot as inevitable, while others don't expect to stay in nursing after marriage, so don't take a long-term view. She has decided to attend union meetings and to be much more active in mobilising and expressing the real feelings of her profession. She says she doesn't delude herself that she's going to have a big impact upon things, at least initially, but she's surprised and pleased at how much better she feels simply from being able to speak up and get her colleagues to think more positively about what they want from the job and what they consider they should and should not be expected to do. She was very gratified to receive a personal reply from her MP to a letter in which she set out nurses' grievances, and she hopes to persuade the MP to visit the hospital for the specific purpose of meeting and talking informally with student nurses.

Encouraging her colleagues to think more closely about their profession and how it should be regarded, has prompted Sandra to look carefully at another item on her list, namely her unrealistically high self-expectations. She realises that part of her has been trying very hard to please, and that this has less to do with what is really expected of her by others than with her attitudes towards herself. Thinking back to childhood, she realises she's always been trying to get others to think well of her, and finds it hard to think well of herself unless they do. She's therefore drawn up her own list of the qualities she thinks a good nurse should have, and finds that she scores quite well on them. She's now determined to discover what it is in herself or in her life experiences that never let her be satisfied with her own performance (see page 56). Half seriously, half jokingly, she's devised several slogans about herself and her work, which she's written out and put on the walls of her room. Her current favourite is 'I don't want to be superwoman, I want to be *ME*!' With her interest in physiology and psychology, Sandra has read about the general adaptation syndrome (see page 11), and uses it to help monitor her stress reactions to the various pressures she has identified in her professional life. She has produced a copy of the GAS for each of these pressures, and has mounted a moveable caricature of herself on each one. She adjusts the position of this caricature forwards and backwards along the GAS line in response to how she feels regarding each stressor from day to day, and says that she hasn't yet in any instance quite been pushed to the

— AVOIDING THE NEED TO PLEASE —

Wanting to please others is a desirable trait. It shows we're concerned for the welfare of those around us, and not too bound up in our own affairs. But there's a big difference between *wanting to please others for their sake*, and *needing to please them in order to satisfy something in ourselves*. Sandra (see page 55) identified the need to please as one of the reasons she's an easy target for stress. She can't think well of herself unless others think well of her, and this means she often makes unrealistically high demands upon herself, feeling that if she falls short of them others will downgrade her in their estimation accordingly. If we're to be ruthless about it, we could say that a need to please of this kind isn't a sign of unselfishness at all, but is simply a way of using others so that we can get to feeling good about ourselves.

The need to please, at least when it's strong as in Sandra's case, usually stems from low self-confidence and an inability to accept ourselves on our own terms. It's a carry-over from childhood, when the child hasn't yet gained enough experience to be objective about him or herself, and is dependent largely upon the judgements and opinions expressed by adults. Adult power to punish through disapproval, and to produce in the child feelings of self-rejection and guilt, multiply the effect.

Strategies for freeing oneself from this childhood conditioning include:

RECOGNISING THE EXISTENCE OF THIS CONDITIONING. It's helpful to think back to experiences within the home and school and identify incidents and relationships in which this conditioning occurred, and thus come to a fuller understanding of our present behaviour and its irrational nature.

PUTTING OURSELVES ON A REWARD SCHEDULE. Many low self-esteem people habitually punish themselves (at a subvocal level) whenever their performance falls below expectations, and dwell subsequently upon these shortcomings. Their strategy should be to concentrate more upon praising themselves when things go well, and starting to think of themselves in terms of success rather than in terms of failure.

BEING MORE REALISTIC IN SELF-EXPECTATIONS. We're familiar enough with the need for realistic expectations when it comes to technical equipment. However good a computer is, there are limits upon what it can do. But when it comes to ourselves we're vague in the extreme about our capacities, and often assume they're unbounded. Try to be as realistic about yourself as you are about your car or your computer!

bottom of the 'exhaustion' slippery slope. She says if nothing else this helps her to stop taking herself quite so seriously, and she's been surprised at how many of her friends have adopted variants of the idea for their own use.

ADDITIONAL STRATEGIES

In addition to illustrating some of the major *knowledge* and *action* issues, Peter and Sandra also show the value of thinking creatively about our response to stressors. If it's true that 'there must be a better way' of handling things, then we have to use our ingenuity to find it. The results may sometimes be quirky and a little idiosyncratic (as with Sandra and her visual trips along the GAS line), but if they make us feel better, that's a good indication they're obeying sound psychological principles, however unlikely this may seem at first sight.

These principles often have to do with *objectifying the problem*. I said that many people find that the very act of making out their list of stressors helps relieve things a little, as they now find their problems have become more tangible. There's also the feeling that in addition to objectifying our problems we've *communicated* them, if only to a piece of paper. The same applies at the action level. Peter's *Rumour Record* for example objectifies and communicates (and shares among colleagues) something of the uncertainty that everyone is experiencing. And Sandra's visual record of her GAS trips has at the personal level the same sort of effect. Instead of seeing our problems as our own fault, objectifying our problems helps us to see them as demands made upon us by the environment (following the definition of stress offered in Chapter 1). This helps us at the practical level to tackle them one by one and work towards their solution.

But of course identifying our problems and deciding what action to take is one thing, carrying the action through is another. Peter and Sandra's brief case studies can't illustrate all the obstacles involved, all the answers to the 'what is stopping me from doing it?' question that we pose during the action stage. Sometimes what stops us is ourselves, and this will be covered in the next chapter. Sometimes what stops us is that our stressors originate from sources that are beyond our power of influence, and these we have to tab 'ignore or adapt to'. Sometimes, however, opposition comes from sources which aren't really part of the stressor at all, but which make their appearance as soon as we're seen to be trying to do something about it. Often chief amongst these are our colleagues, because dealing with our stressors means changing our behaviour in some way and this change can be threatening for others. Colleagues may have stressors enough of their own, and may get the uncomfortable feeling that less stress for us may mean more stress for them!

HOW TO MANAGE COLLEAGUES' OPPOSITION

Often opposition from colleagues surfaces not when we're proposing changes that will affect everyone. These are matters for debate, and, like Peter's suggestions for improving the communications network, stand a good chance of commanding general support if they're seen to be beneficial. It surfaces when we make changes that directly affect only ourselves. Smokers trying to give up smoking say that frequently their worst obstacles are friends still hooked on the habit. Maybe these friends feel jealous of someone strong enough to do what they would all secretly like to do. Maybe they just feel there's safety in numbers. But they exert all kinds of subtle pressures upon the escapee to rejoin them in prison. In the end, the escapee is made to feel somewhat ostracised by the bid for freedom, and may backslide just for the comfort of once more being one of the crowd.

In a not dissimilar way, the stress reducer may be made subtly to feel that he or she is letting the side down, and had much better go back to old chaotic work practices. This feeling is usually only temporary, and endures only until everyone has become used to his or her new ways, but it's uncomfortable while it's there, and may well prove a powerful disincentive. So take the following steps to avoid it.

INFORM PEOPLE OF THE CHANGES YOU'RE GOING TO MAKE WHEREVER THESE ARE LIKELY TO BE APPARENT

For instance, if you're only going to be available to colleagues at certain set times, send a note round to this effect. If you're not going to stay in the office after the end of the working day, tell people about it. If you're going to take a short coffee break in your room each morning instead of a longer one in the staff canteen, tell them about that too. Give your reasons, so that people will be reassured there's nothing personal about any of your decisions. An added bonus of publicising your new working practices is that it gives you a powerful incentive to stick to them. Too many people will be lying in wait to say 'I *knew* you'd never keep it up' for you to give in easily.

BE FIRM ABOUT THESE CHANGES

There are plenty of people around who think that none of your changes apply in practice to them, or that you'll be only too pleased to make an exception just this once. As I say in Chapter 5, learning how to say 'no' and mean it is an essential personal quality in resisting stress, and you really have to apply this learning now. Once you make one exception, you'll quickly be making two or three, and find yourself fiercely resented by anyone who isn't extended this privilege.

DRAW COLLEAGUES INTO THESE CHANGES WHERE POSSIBLE

Wherever you can, try and make your changes benefit others as well as yourself. The best way to do this is on a contractual basis, so that each of you is able to support the other. This creates a *mutual support group*, with each member agreeing to change in ways that are mutually beneficial, or, where this isn't possible, to respect each other's changes and agree to abide by them.

ENSURE YOUR CHANGES KEEP A BALANCE BETWEEN WITHDRAWING FROM THE ENVIRONMENT AND MOVING TOWARDS IT

If all your changes are of the 'not available to colleagues' variety, you end up isolated and without the opportunities for this kind of mutual support group. If you can't make your changes mutually beneficial, at least ensure that they don't take you too far into your own shell. Build into your programme a time when you *can* be with others, and regard this as every bit as vital as your other stress reduction strategies. Studies show that people who are introverted tend to seek solitude when troubled, while those who are extraverted seek company. I'm not arguing against this pattern. But the company of others and communication with them is of value even to stressed introverts. Talking to others helps to put problems into perspective, to invite suggestions for their solution, and to feel social warmth and sympathy.

ACT RATHER THAN REACT

Even where it isn't clear what changes you should make, this doesn't mean you should lower your guard so to speak. Life is a constant process of change, and this applies as much to our professional lives as to our biological and psychological ones. You're never exempt from organisational changes that are likely to affect you, and many of these may serve to increase rather than decrease your stress. Be on the alert for these changes, and try to do something about them before they and their consequences become irrevocable facts. Predict them where you can, and take the initiative in acting. People who in their professional

ARE YOU AN ACTOR OR A REACTOR?

Actors (the term has nothing to do with the stage!) tend not to be caught napping by events. They show:

▶ **Powers of anticipation.** They identify what is likely to happen, and take steps to avoid it or profit from it or change it to suit their own interests. They tend to be well-informed and in the right place at the right time. Sometimes for this reason they are unfairly described as 'lucky' by their acquaintances.

▶ **Decisiveness.** They make up their minds what to do while others are still deliberating. Generally this isn't the same as being impulsive. Impulsive people are those who don't anticipate, and who act hastily when the 'danger' is almost upon them.

▶ **Courage.** Acting quickly and decisively often involves an element of perceived risk. They are prepared to take this risk, while others delay around them (and in the long run perhaps incur even greater risk).

▶ **Good stress resistance.** Actors are often able to stay with the stress, and keep a keen eye on how things are turning out, when highly stressed individuals are taking refuge in escape or denial ('It won't really come to a crisis.' 'Things will sort themselves out.' 'I've just got to get away from it all.').

This doesn't mean that actors are 'better' people than reactors. They may be opportunist, self-centred, and even ruthless. On the other hand reactors may be indecisive and ineffectual, and end up consistently stressed by their inability to control events. Ideal behaviour therefore involves the ability both to act and react, dependent upon the demands of the situation and the legitimate rights of other people and of yourself.

In terms of the four qualities listed above, assess whether you're an actor or a reactor, and how this influences the levels of stress in your life. If you miss out by being a reactor, assess whether changing your behaviour to that of an actor will lead to more, or less stress. If you do want to act rather than react, *look ahead, be well informed*, and stay with difficult situations instead of trying to escape from them.

lives seem always to be at the mercy of circumstances are usually those who wait for things to happen, and then *react* to them. People who seem more on top of things are usually those who see things coming, and *act* in good time to guard against them (or benefit from them).

ENVIRONMENTAL VERSUS PERSONAL CAUSES OF STRESS

So much then for the stressors that come about through the demands of the environment. The next chapter switches focus to the inner qualities that determine how we respond to these stressors, and focuses as well upon those stressors that we actually invent for ourselves. We can't make a clear distinction between what goes on outside us and how we respond to it, but the example in Chapter 1 of the sound of footsteps in an 'empty' house showed how important our cognitive appraisals are in determining whether events trigger off our emotional responses or not. We'll now investigate *what it is in us* that makes us perceive things as stressful or not, and *what it is in us* that determines whether we can handle this stress or not. And as you may have guessed, the next chapter starts by returning briefly to our Zen friend and his wild strawberries.

Chapter Five

What Causes Too Much Stress?

— you yourself

It was clear that our strawberry-eating friend could do very little about his environmental stressors. Poised increasingly precariously between the tiger above and the tiger below, he could do nothing to free himself and get back to life as he used to know it. Yet unperturbed, he was able not only to spot the wild strawberries but to eat them and actually find them enjoyable. So what was his secret? Clearly he had tabbed the two tigers, the drop to the cliff bottom, and the activities of the two mice as 'ignore or adapt to'. He could neither escape from them nor do anything to affect them, so he refused to allow them to trouble him. *But how?* It's easy enough to say, as I did in the last chapter, that Sandra is working on her 'ignore' skills. We'd most of us agree that, assuming there was no one within earshot to hear his cries, our strawberry-eating friend was sensible to relish the taste of his strawberries while he could, but if we were in his position could we do the same? Would we be able to show his good sense and his equanimity?

Which brings us back to his secret. Why was he able to behave as he did, while most of us would be wasting our last moments on earth in unavailing screams and struggles?

COGNITIVE APPRAISALS

Part of the answer lies in the power of our cognitive appraisals to influence our emotions. We hear a set of footsteps upstairs. If we think they are those of an intruder, we panic. If we think they are those of our partner, we relax. Same footsteps, two quite different responses dependent upon the way in which we cognitively appraise or interpret them. The situation is rather more complex with our strawberry-eating friend, but the principle remains the same. Certainly his first appraisal would be that he was in grave danger, but his second appraisal could *either* be that therefore he must panic, *or* that if he had only a short few minutes left to live, he ought to regard them as infinitely precious, and therefore make the very most of them.

Grasping the full significance of the power of cognitive appraisals over our emotions means realising that we *can* use our thoughts to influence how we feel. This isn't the same as saying it's easy to do so, but it's a vital statement which we must understand if we are to develop our power to withstand stress. And lest we think the Zen story isn't a fair way of illustrating this, since it comes from the East and Easterners are believed to have a more 'fatalistic' approach to life (only another way of saying that they are brought up with different sets of cognitive appraisals from Westerners) let me quote Epictetus, one of the founding fathers of stoicism, who argued that 'men are not disquieted by things themselves, *but by their idea of things*'. We may not be able to match Epictetus, who exemplified in his wise and noble life the profound psychological insights that underpinned his philosophy (psychology is by no means the exclusive preserve of modern psychologists!), but we can at least ponder the implications of what he says for human behaviour.

Having accepted these implications what next? People are prone to say of a stressor 'Yes I know it's silly to let it get me down, but I can't help it', or 'One part of me knows there's no point in getting into a state about it, but another part of me just can't stop'. The correct cognitive appraisal seems to be there, but it clearly isn't getting through to where it matters, the emotional trigger mechanism. 'I know nobody can hear me, but I can't stop yelling'.

Clearly what's happening is that we haven't fully accepted the cognitive appraisal. We hear footsteps and are sure at one level they belong to our partner, but at another level some part of us is unconvinced. Or we know it's no good struggling to get back to the cliff top and to evade the tiger, but our fight or flight mechanism struggles on, even though our struggles make us ignore the strawberries (and probably only send us to our doom all the quicker). Once we've made the correct appraisals, therefore, we need to find ways of *schooling* ourselves so that these appraisals are allowed to have their proper say over how we respond. Constantly alerting our emotions and our physiological system to fight battles we can't win or aren't even allowed to fight, or to run away when circumstances keep us rooted to the spot, is what wears down our resistance and pushes us ultimately to the stage of collapse on the GAS line.

This schooling is discussed in Chapter 6, but first must be emphasised the part cognitive appraisals play in any stress-reduction programme. One set of cognitive appraisals has to do with environmental stressors, and we've already looked at these and seen how we should tab them for action or for ignoring. But another set of appraisals has to do with the way in which we understand ourselves and our own reactions to things. What is it *in us* that determines how we respond to the pressures which the environment places upon us? How well do we know ourselves, and recognise the nature of our responses and why they're happening? And how aware are we of (and prepared to acknowledge) our personal idiosyncracies, our personal foibles and likes and dislikes which, though apparently minor in themselves, nevertheless profoundly influence our habitual ways of responding?

Sit down and make an inventory of the things about yourself that seem to make you susceptible to unnecessary stress. Personalise the inventory by starting each item with 'I'. This helps you to *own* the items. You're writing about yourself, not about someone else, and there's no need to be diffident or ashamed of any of the qualities you're recognising in yourself.

Jane: a case study of personal causes of stress

❏ Jane, who has a degree in mathematics, and who two years after graduation is working for a very busy firm of computer consultants in London, came up with the following list. She was asked to head it with a simple statement which she considered summed up what she was writing about.

Reasons why I'm an easy target

– *I let myself get manoeuvred into false positions*
– *I react rather than act*
– *I'm taken by surprise by opposition or anger in others*
– *I get easily upset*
– *I hate noise and muddle*
– *I hate being asked to do two things at once*
– *I find it hard to say 'no' when asked to do something*
– *I want to be liked*
– *I'm always speculating on other people's motives when I'm with them*
– *I write things down on scraps of paper instead of having a proper system (and I'm supposed to be a computer expert!)*

– I daydream in meetings
– I don't feel I'm appreciated by my boss
– I resent it that other people in the office, who were not trained as
  mathematicians, seem to think they know as much about maths as I
  do
– I find it hard to speak up for myself when there are men in the group.

Discussing her list, Jane said how surprised she was that the simple exercise of having to sit down and write it out had taught her more about herself in five minutes than she'd learnt during her previous two years in her job. Or at least, it had made her admit to things about herself that up to now she'd not really recognised. She described herself as moderately stressed in her professional and in her personal life, but had the feeling that things were tending to get worse as she grew older rather than better. When asked to rate the other people in her office and her personal friends as either 'more, or less, stressed than me' Jane rated the majority of them as 'less stressed', and said that generally she felt they were 'more together' than she was. She was interested to learn that when a sample of her colleagues was asked to carry out the same exercise, the majority rated Jane as *less* stressed than they were themselves, thus reversing her own view of things.

Looking through Jane's inventory, we can see that some of the items on it are straightforward enough. Perhaps many of us have a tendency to daydream in meetings if we find them uninteresting, even though this means we may miss important issues, and be subsequently stressed by our lack of vital pieces of information or by the realisation that we failed to see the full implication of decisions that were being taken and let slip the chance of influencing them. And we perhaps many of us react rather than act (see Chapter 4), or make notes on scraps of paper or perhaps rely on our memories when we should be operating an efficient store/retrieval system. But there are other things on Jane's inventory that need more discussion. Her tendency to be manoeuvred into false positions for example, or her inability to say 'no' when demands are made of her, or her difficulty in speaking up in male company or her wish to be liked. Together, these give a picture of someone who is rather unsure of herself, and lacks the confidence to assert herself and her own views and her own rights. This lack of confidence is further demonstrated by her ratings of her colleagues and friends as generally less stressed than herself, though the fact that they see her rather differently suggests she doesn't very often communicate her real feelings to others, and mostly appears more self-assured than she actually is. Since she specifies that it is in the presence of men

LEARNING TO SAY NO WHEN NECESSARY

People who find it hard to say 'no' when demands, however
unreasonable, are made of them, usually put this down to one or
more of the following reasons:

* They lack confidence in their own powers of
  judgement as to what they should and should not be
  expected to do.

* They are anxious to be liked and afraid others will
  think badly of them if they refuse to do as they're
  requested.

* They have only a hazy idea of how many duties and
  tasks they can successfully take on.

* They have a well-developed conscience, and feel
  guilty if they 'refuse to help'.

* They feel inferior to other people and see them as
  having 'authority' over them.

But whatever their reason, people who can't say no usually
confess to being overtaken by events. They tend to be reactors
rather than actors (see page 60). In spite of past experiences,
they never have an answer ready when requests are put to them.
   If you find it hard to say no even when you know your refusal is
perfectly justified, use these points to help you:

* Anticipate the occasions when someone is likely to
  make an unacceptable demand upon you. Be ready
  for him or her.

* Rehearse your answers to yourself. Have three or
  four set forms of words which you can use (e.g.
  'Sorry I'm just having to say "no" to that these days;
  I'm over my ears in work.') and *practice them out
  loud to yourself*.

* Don't make excuses when you say 'no'. If you have
  a reason for your refusal and you want to give it,
  fine. Keep it short and to the point. But you don't
  have to give a reason. You've a perfect right to say
  'no' if you want to do so.

* When you've said 'no', stick to it. If you vacilate,
  people will soon get the idea that they can work on
  you to change your mind.

* When you've said 'no', *don't feel guilty about it*.
  You're the best judge of what you can and can't be
  expected to do.

that she feels special difficulty in speaking up for herself, it's probable that her sex plays some part in matters, since society traditionally assigns women an inferior role from which they often have to struggle hard both with themselves and with others to escape.

Jane also has some other revealing details on her inventory. For example, she tells of her habit of speculating about other people's motives when they're with her. It was particularly perceptive of her to identify this as a stressor, and she amplified this verbally by saying that she often found herself worrying that people were getting at her when in fact they'd probably only made a chance, innocent remark. Or worrying that they were trying to outshine her in their work, when doubtless they were far too bound up in what they were doing even to give her a second thought. The more she thought about this, the more she was convinced that it was one of the major reasons why sometimes she finished the day feeling so tense and tearful.

Other significant items in Jane's inventory are her recognition that she's easily upset and that she's caught unawares by other people's opposition or anger. Being easily upset is partly to do with temperament. From babyhood onwards some people are more prone to tears and emotional hurt than others. But however easily upset we are, we have to *identify* things as threatening before our emotions are actually triggered. So Jane was asked what kinds of thing upset her, and after some thought she linked most of them back to the earlier discussion about low self-esteem. Feelings of being rejected or misunderstood or unfairly criticised by others upset her most, since they threatened the good opinion she was trying, not very successfully, to have of herself. She felt that constantly being caught off-guard by other people's antagonism was perhaps part and parcel of the same thing. Her need to be liked by those around her was so strong that, although not a selfish person, she focused so much on her own feelings and upon what others thought of her that she missed opportunities to study them objectively, and predict how they were going to respond. In a way, she confessed, she just wasn't very realistic about others. And whenever people became angry, she always took it personally, instead of seeing their anger as a routine reaction to the stress that *they* happened to be feeling.

Finally, Jane recognised that her impression her boss undervalued her, and that her colleagues weren't giving her enough credit for her degree in mathematics, might either be true or simply another aspect of her need for acceptance. She resolved to look more closely at these two things in future, and firstly to record the occasions both when her boss signalled approval of her and the occasions when approval was justified but wasn't forthcoming; and secondly to record the occasions when her colleagues signalled they thought they knew as much about mathematics as she did. By analysing her records, she would be able to decide whether her resentment over these matters was appropriate or not.

ALTERING YOUR COGNITIVE APPRAISALS

Once Jane has recognised what it is in herself that, in her own words, makes her an easy target, she can explore whether things can be changed simply by altering the cognitive appraisals associated with them. Daydreaming in meetings and writing things down on scraps of paper instead of taking the trouble to record them properly indicates that, deep down she isn't *really* appraising the events concerned as important enough. If she fully accepted that what happened in meetings had an important bearing upon her job, and that the time taken to record information properly was much briefer than the frantic minutes spent hunting for her illusive scraps of paper, then she would have a strong incentive to change her working habits.

Similarly, if her cognitive appraisal of herself was based upon actual current facts (her good degree in mathematics, her skill at her job, her ability to get on well with people) rather than upon thought patterns carried over from what she admits was a somewhat loveless and difficult childhood, her self-concepts and self-esteem would change in positive directions. This would help her to be more confident and self-assertive, less easily manoeuvred into false positions, less dependent upon the good opinion of others, less emotionally threatened, and more able to say 'no' and to stand her ground when necessary.

And a more accurate appraisal of her working conditions would prompt her to see that having to do two things at once and having to work in a hectic and at times chaotic environment were inseparable from the kind of job she had chosen to do. Things of this kind would therefore just have to be tabbed 'ignore or adapt to'. Maybe she still has a rather unrealistic, even idealistic, view of her job, and this will need to be brought more in line with reality if she is to give herself a proper chance of relaxing into it and enjoying it rather more.

TEMPERAMENT AND STRESS

I've said that Jane's tendency to be easily upset is partly due to her temperament. But temperament can render us over-susceptible to stress for reasons other than extreme sensitivity.

Bernard: a case study of personal causes of stress

❏ Bernard is chief adviser to a busy local education authority. His job means that he has responsibility for a team of advisers, covering most areas of the school curriculum, who are charged with the job of monitoring the effectiveness of much of what goes on in the classroom, and advising teachers on new ideas and new teaching methods in their respective subjects. Bernard is in his mid-fifties, with a grown-up family and a wife who is a primary school headteacher in a neighbouring local authority. Bernard confesses to being a workaholic. He prides himself on being in his office by 8 o'clock every morning, and seldom leaves before 6 or 7 p.m. He takes work home with him most evenings and weekends, and boasts that he drives his staff hard, and is impatient with any signs of weakness or inefficiency. Because no one can match up to his standards, he hates delegating, and takes all the major decisions himself. He has little time for physical exercise (beyond running furiously up and down stairs when the lifts at city hall are too slow in coming), and no time at all for hobbies or leisure interests. He describes his work as his life, and is rather pleased by the fact that he's generally rather unpopular with his staff of advisers and with teachers in school. He sees this as a sign of how effective he is at his work, and is probably accurate when he says that though he may be disliked, he's certainly widely respected.

Bernard talks rapidly and jerkily, and tends to interrupt others or finish sentences for them if they don't put forward their ideas as quickly as he does himself. It's noticeable that except when he wants specific pieces of information, he asks very few questions, preferring to make statements or to press his own point of view. He isn't averse to listening to jokes, provided they are short and quickly come to the punch line, but for the most part his approach to life is unremittingly serious and purposeful. He expressed considerable surprise when asked whether he enjoyed his work, and made it clear that he thought this was a rather silly question. Work was there to be done, not necessarily to become ecstatic about.

'TYPE A' PERSONALITIES

Bernard is, of course, a prime example of what psychologists and medical doctors have come to call the 'Type A' personality. Type A individuals are competitive, hard-driving, impatient and rather inflexible in their approach. Heavily involved in their work (a characteristic known as *involved striving*), they like deadlines and pressures, prefer to lead rather than to be led, and are more anxious for approval by superiors than for peer approval. Though often aware of being burdened by their work load (*environmental overburdening*) they show little signs of sympathy towards themselves, and are no more tolerant with their own weaknesses than they are with those in other people.

Bernard and other Type A personalities would tend to answer 'yes' to the majority of the following questions:

Type A personality questionnaire

	Yes	No
1. Do you characteristically do several things at once (e.g. telephoning, holding a conversation, jotting notes on a pad and swivelling back and forth on your chair all at the same time)?	□	□
2. Do you feel guilty when relaxing, as if there's always something else you should be doing?	□	□
3. Are you quickly bored when other people are talking? Do you find yourself wanting to interrupt, or finish their sentences for them, or in some way get them to hurry up?	□	□
4. Do you try to steer conversations towards your own interests, instead of wanting to hear about those of others?	□	□
5. Are you usually anxious when engaged in a task to get it finished so that you can get on to the next job?	□	□

	Yes	No
6. Are you unobservant when it comes to anything that isn't immediately connected with what you're actually doing?	☐	☐
7. Do you prefer to *have* rather than to *be* (i.e. to experience your possessions rather than to experience yourself)?	☐	☐
8. Do you do most things (eating, talking, walking) at top speed?	☐	☐
9. Do you find people like yourself challenging and people who dawdle infuriating?	☐	☐
10. Are you physically tense and assertive?	☐	☐
11. Are you more interested in winning than simply in taking part and enjoying yourself?	☐	☐
12. Do you find it hard to laugh at yourself?	☐	☐
13. Do you find it hard to delegate?	☐	☐
14. Do you find it almost impossible to attend meetings without speaking up?	☐	☐
15. Do you prefer activity holidays to dreamy, relaxing ones?	☐	☐
16. Do you push those for whom you're responsible (children, subordinates, partner) to try to achieve your own standards, without showing much interest in what *they* really want out of life?	☐	☐

score

Extreme Type A people score 16 'yes' responses out of 16, but many people who get less than a full score nevertheless answer 'yes' often enough to indicate they have significant Type A tendencies. Some studies show a correlation between Type A behaviour and coronary disease, high blood pressure and strokes. The Type A personality seems to have his or her citizen army (of Chapter 1) mobilised almost permanently for action, usually in the fight rather than flight direction, and find it difficult to stand this army down and relax or even *want* to do so.

There certainly seems to be a strong temperamental factor at work here, in that some people are by nature more assertive, competitive and goal-orientated than others, but learning also plays an important part.

Bernard recalls that during his childhood his parents were always pushing him to higher and higher levels of achievement. To obtain their approval, he had to be top. If he came home from school and announced he'd got good marks for his work, before praising him his father or mother would always ask if those were the best marks in the class. If they weren't, then no matter how good the marks, praise would always be slow in coming, or qualified by the rider that next time he shouldn't let so-and-so beat him. When he played sport for the school, his father would faithfully attend all matches, and bellow at him from the touchline to make more and more effort. If he had a poor game, his father wouldn't speak to him on the journey home.

Talking about these early experiences, Bernard clearly approves of them, and says they've helped him to get where he is. He admits to driving his own children equally hard, and when discussing the quality of the schools under his charge he's quick to quote detailed statistics on examination successes, and to cite improvement in these statistics as the best proof that he and his team of advisers are succeeding in pushing up the quality of education in the city. He shows himself disinclined to discuss criteria other than examination results, though he is also quick to quote the numbers of teachers who attend in-service courses in the city and other facts and figures designed to show that the advisory service is working well.

Unlike Jane, Bernard isn't keen on making an inventory of the things in his own behaviour that make him a target for stress. He blames it all on the constraints in the system within which he has to work, and the delays and frustrations caused by inefficiency and woolly thinking on the part of others. Generally, he feels the answer is that people, from politicians in the Department of Education and Science down to school cleaners, should demand more of themselves, cut out indecision, and bring more urgency into what they have to do.

— MANAGING TYPE A BEHAVIOUR —

If, like Bernard, you score highly on the Type A Personality Questionnaire (page 70), try introducing more Type B personality behaviour into your life. This means taking each item in the Questionnaire and producing the behaviours that would allow you to answer 'no' in response to it. Easy enough in theory, but much harder in practice. Many Type A personalities often argue, like Bernard, that they just don't want to change. Or that everything would be fine if only other people would stop being so inefficient.

So the first step is to accept that Type A behaviour is doing *physiological* damage to you. Re-read the relevant details in Chapter 1. Most Type A individuals are high on achievement motivation. They want to get things done. And once they allow themselves to adopt a goal of greater physical fitness and health, they can become very single-minded in pursuing it. Even to the extent of watching their behaviour much more closely and making determined efforts to change it. Since they like to see tangible results, it's helpful if they can have some objective measure of their improvement in performance. Lower resting pulse rate for example, lower blood pressure, more miles jogged or cycled or registered on an exercise bike in a given time etc. And, if possible, a reduced blood cholesterol level.

The most obvious areas of behaviour for a Type A personality to change are usually to do with:

▶ *Humour.* Type A people need to laugh more, particularly at themselves. To stand back a little and see the funny side of all their *involved striving* for example.

▶ *Wider horizons*. Type A's are prone to be much too bound up in their work. More time spent developing other interests is vital (see also *If you're an over-identifier*, page 77).

▶ *More understanding of others*. Many Type A's just don't realise that other people are different from themselves in temperament, values, ambitions etc. A little time spent appreciating others more, and the right of others to be different, is essential.

▶ *More delegation. Type A's should understand the value to self and others of judicial delegation. They can't do everything themselves.

▶ *Relaxed time schedules.* Type A's need to do everything a little slower. Ease off on deadlines. Walk and move and talk slower. Become more conscious of their jerky, hectic approach to life, and consciously ease back on themselves.

▶ *Patience towards oneself and towards others.* Type A's need to study themselves more, instead of simply making demands on themselves. To listen more to others. To let others have their say without interrupting. To become more aware of the need to *be* instead of always to *do*, the need to *enjoy* instead of simply to *have*.

OTHER PERSONAL CAUSES OF STRESS

In addition to those that make, in their different ways, Jane and Bernard targets for stress, there are a number of other personal qualities that deserve mention.

OBSESSIONALITY

There are certain signs of obsessionality in Bernard, but this characteristic isn't simply confined to Type A personalities. When we think of obsessionality, we usually picture the obsessional neurotic, an individual who is so governed by his or her obsessions that the whole day is spent in meaningless rituals (such as compulsive hand washing, or house cleaning, or in attempts to avoid contact with anything that carries associations with toileting or sexuality). But the obsessional *neurotic* and the obsessional *personality* are recognised by psychologists as two distinct cases. Both are controlled by their obsessions, but whereas to the former these obsessions are a source of suffering and a handicap to normal living, to the latter they are a source of pride and often confer certain advantages. On the one hand we have the ritualistic hand-washer, and on the other we have the meticulous secretary or the single-minded industrialist. The evidence doesn't suggest that the obsessional personality develops into the obsessional neurotic. The two conditions seem to remain functionally distinct from each other.

But unless the environment dovetails with their obsessionality, obsessional personalities can find themselves constantly fighting a battle to make it do so. Focused as they are upon the subject of their obsessionality, they cannot grasp the fact that there are other interests to be studied in addition to their own; that other people also have preferences and opinions and ways of doing things, and have equal rights to have their individuality respected. Neither can they grasp the fact that the world wasn't designed specifically for the convenience of their obsessions, and often just doesn't behave in the neat and ordered way that they might like.

We saw a small instance of this in Jane's dislike of muddle, and suggested that (assuming she couldn't set the muddle straight) she'd do far better to realise that muddle was a part of her job, and that she has to learn to live with it. But the true obsessional personality is much more fixed in his or her thinking than Jane. Often he or she is deeply unhappy in an environment where everything isn't cut and dried, precise and predictable. In practice this means that many obsessionals have a low tolerance of ambiguity, and since tolerance of ambiguity is a necessary feature of certain kinds of creative activity, this means that their creative impulses aren't given proper scope for development. They may also feel a strong resistance to change, to radical thinking, to new challenges, with the result that obsessionals will find certain kinds of job very unsettling, frustrating and stressful. Given an environment which supports their obsessions, obsessional personalities may be very successful indeed. Given an environment that fails to do so, they may find the going very hard.

LOW RISK TAKING AND SENSATION SEEKING

I mentioned in Chapter 1 that we all need a certain level of stress if we're not to become bored and unhappy. The required level varies from person to person, and also varies in terms of the *kind* of stress required. People high on qualities which psychologists call *risk taking* and *sensation seeking* respectively, need plenty of challenges and hazards to get their pulses racing and to put them into a state of high arousal. But for *low* risk takers and *low* sensation seekers, a job which carries these factors will be disastrously stressful. They will find it well-nigh impossible to cope for long with the constant jolts to the nervous system which challenges and risks carry with them. And incidentally, there's even a limit to how long the high risk takers and sensation seekers can stand the pace if it's unremitting enough, as witness for example the alleged early burn-out rate of highly pressurised financial wizards in the hot-house world of international money and futures markets.

OVER-IDENTIFICATION

Most people derive much of their identity from the jobs they do. Ask them who they are, and after giving you their names and perhaps their family status many of them will offer their professions as a means of self-definition. This is, of course, one reason why many people find retirement stressful, since it involves them in abruptly relinquishing part of their identity, and often at a time when they are no longer easily able to create a new persona in its place. But *over-identification* with one's employment means that even when still working, one is highly vulnerable to anything that casts doubt on one's professional competence. To the over-identifier, any doubt on this competence casts doubt on one's value as a person, and is therefore both threatening and stressful. To the over-identifier, promotion to higher levels is, not surprisingly, valued less for the increased job satisfaction it brings (it may bring quite the reverse), than for the reassurance that one is an effective and worthwhile person.

Over-identifiers may be obsessionals, Type A personalities, lonely people for whom the job compensates for lack of family and friends, or simply insecure people who aren't too sure of their identity and need their job to give them standing in their own eyes and in those of their fellows. But the consequence of over-identification is that individuals become (dependent upon temperament) either very aggressive or defensive if their professional pride is challenged, and find themselves embroiled all too often in unnecessary and wounding battles. Often their very attitude invites attack from others. The schoolteacher is sometimes a particular example of this. Investing too much of oneself in professional dignity and status is an open challenge to children to reduce one to size. The more outraged and offended one becomes, the worse the children get. 'Do you know what the little brats said to *me*?' shouts the mortally insulted teacher to colleagues in the staff common-room, or 'Do you know what the blighters have been calling *me* behind my back?'. Minor incidents which other teachers take as a routine part of school life are blown up out of all proportion. Trivial acts of disobedience which the wise teacher knows are best ignored are turned into major incidents. Small clashes of temperament are exaggerated into major confrontations. The teacher invests so much of him or herself into the role, that objectivity and the ability to laugh at oneself are submerged under a sea of accusations and recriminations.

BLAMING YOURSELF

Sometimes it is we who are to blame for what goes wrong in our professional lives, sometimes it's the system, sometimes it's someone else. The mature individual is able to be objective and assign blame where it rightfully belongs. But if we can't do this, we at once increase our susceptibility to stress. This is particularly true where we persist in blaming ourselves for things that are in fact largely outside our control. Everything that goes wrong we lay at our own door. We should have foreseen the emergency. We should have taken proper steps to prevent it. We should have kept quiet. Or we should have spoken out. Or we should have been more fully committed. Or we should have worked harder. The excuses for blaming ourselves can be endless. What's happening of course is that we're carrying into our professional lives (into our adult lives in general for that matter) a pattern of thinking acquired in childhood. Children often lack the experience to be objective about matters, and are all too easily conditioned into

── IF YOU'RE AN OVER-IDENTIFIER ──

Over-identification with one's job develops subtly and insidiously.
Many people confess to not realising quite how strong this
identification has become until they're made redundant, retired, or
moved into a different form of employment. When these changes
happen they find themselves devastated, no longer sure who they
are or what use they are to themselves or anyone else.

☐ Over-identification means that a major part of our sense of
significance and self-worth has become bound up in the job.
Even when we meet people outside the context of work, there is
a strong sense in which we're relating to them not in terms of
who we are and what we have to offer at that particular moment,
but in terms of our job label. The prouder we are of that label,
and the more we enjoy our work, the greater the chances of this
happening. Even if we don't introduce work-related topics into
the conversation, we still think of our personal and social status
viz-a-viz other people in terms of our label. The opposite can
happen if we *aren't* very proud of our job. In this case, we
downgrade ourselves viz-a-viz others, and are very anxious to
keep the topic of conversation away from work and onto more
neutral grounds.

☐ Examine the extent to which you over-identify by carrying out a
simple, but quite challenging exercise. Write down as many
responses as you can to the repeated question 'Who am I?'.
The number of responses is less important than the nature of
them. Examine your list when you've finished. How strongly does
your job feature within it? How *do* you define yourself? Is it in
terms of things? of people? of past history? of future ambitions?
How much of *yourself* is in the definition? Your personal qualities,
your values, your attitudes? Is there any reference to the way in
which you *experience* yourself? Your emotions, your inner states
of mind?

☐ If it's clear from this exercise that much of who you are is bound
up in the job, think what this means in terms of making you
vulnerable to stress. A measure of identification with the job is
good, too much causes problems. Redress the balance by finding
more of yourself in your family and friends, in your interests
outside work, in getting to know what you really want from life
and what you see as its purpose. Remember that, for one reason
or another, you're going to have to give up your job one day.
What will be left of you when this happens?

thinking that they're the ones who are always in the wrong. Over-censorious parents and teachers leave the child thinking that whether the actual reasons are apparent or not, the fault for whatever goes wrong always rests on his or her shoulders.

The reverse of the coin is represented by children who are always allowed to get away with blaming other people for their own short-comings. They may then encounter stress in adult life because they cannot accept when they themselves are at fault, and therefore blame the environment for errors which they could quickly avoid or rectify if they were prepared to acknowledge their own involvement and change their behaviour accordingly. Tendencies to attribute the cause of our life situation to ourselves on the one hand, or to the environment on the other, are referred to by psychologists as *internal locus of control* and *external locus of control* respectively. Someone with an internal locus of control is more likely to attribute success to his or her own efforts ('I did well because I worked hard'), while someone whose locus of control is external will more often attribute success to the environment ('I had the lucky breaks'). As with apportioning blame, both these tendencies can have their drawbacks if they prevent the individual from being properly objective about what is happening.

SEXUAL STEREOTYPING

The evidence isn't very clear on which sex copes better with stress. This is because individual differences and the range of potential stres-sors themselves are so great that crude divisions along sex lines aren't always very helpful. Statistics show that whereas the incidence of emotional disorders is higher in women, premature deaths from so-called stress-related physical illness (heart attacks, strokes) are more common among men.

Sexual stereotyping places different kinds of stress upon the two sexes, and also allows different kinds of stress response from them. Women face far more stress in terms of poor status, uncertainty, powerlessness (which includes sexual harassment), and lack of variety (probably also time pressures, where these involve clashes between domestic and professional responsibilities). Men on the other hand face more stress caused by unsociable hours, clashes with superiors, conflicts with colleagues, and job responsibilities. So far as responses to stress are concerned, women are usually allowed more scope for tears, withdrawal, absenteeism and weakness generally (flight res-ponses) and men more scope for anger, aggression and self-assertion (fight responses).

In handling stress, it's important to identify when these sexual stereotypes are implicated in our problems. In simple terms, women may be stressed by the insufficient importance given by society to values traditionally recognised as 'feminine', and by the simultaneous refusal by society to allow women to develop the more 'masculine' side of their natures. And men may be stressed by society's over-emphasis upon 'masculine' values, and by its reluctance to allow men to develop the more 'feminine' side of their natures. Women have traditionally to be meek, subservient, and content always to be led rather than to lead, while men have traditionally to be tough, aggressive, and ready to lead rather than to be led. Women can cry and attract sympathy through helplessness, but not get angry or expect equality of status and professional prospects with men. Men can get angry and attract respect through mastery, but can't cry or expect magnanimity from others in defeat.

Sexual stereotyping may be breaking down a little in modern society, but the process is very slow, and still leaves men dominating the positions of power in virtually every walk of life. This places strains upon both sexes, and rather in the way that the physical body hasn't yet adapted to the fact that we no longer need high-energy physical responses in the face of threat (see Chapter 1), so society hasn't adapted to the fact that it no longer needs male-dominated behaviour throughout the corridors of power.

STRESS IN THE HOME

Many people find it much harder to be objective about the causes of domestic stress than about stress at work. This is because their emotional involvement with what's happening within the home is that much greater. As I said at the end of Chapter 4, it isn't easy for example to admit that someone as close to one's heart as a partner or a child is instrumental in making life difficult. But if you're as serious about tackling unwanted stress in the home as you are about tackling it in other areas of your life, there's no escape from being honest with yourself or ultimately with the rest of your family.

Kath and Graham: a case study of stress in the home

❏ Kath and Graham both lead busy professional lives, have a son
   Nicholas in his first year at school, and are struggling to make

mortgage repayments on their house. Although they both
enjoy their work and describe their partnership as a good one,
they own up to finding life on top of them most of the time.
Kath describes herself as 'constantly on edge', and Graham as
'just depressed a lot of the time'. Both say they feel chronically
tired, explained partly by the long hours they work and the
plentiful late evenings spent with friends.

After some hesitation, Kath and Graham both set aside time
to look at their lives, and to identify stressors at work and
within the home. We needn't follow up what they had to say
about work, but within the home they surprised themselves by
the number of things that went into their list. Some of the most
important were:

PARTNER STRESS

Top of Kath's list was Graham's reluctance to help in the home. It was
only when she allowed herself to think calmly about it that she realised
how much she resented this reluctance, and how it seemed to say
something threatening about their relationship ('As if deep down he
doesn't really value me'). Among her subsidiary problems were Graham's willingness to let his mates descend upon them at all hours and
raid the fridge for beer and snacks, and the regularity with which he
wiped the answering machine clean and forgot to pass on the telephone messages that had come for her.

Graham's list started with the grouses that Kath was a sight too
friendly towards other men at parties, left everything to the last
minute, and had furious tidying binges which involved putting his
things in places where he could never find them.

CHILD STRESS

Both Kath and Graham agreed that stress over Nicholas amounted
mainly to feelings of guilt that they were neglecting him. He wasn't
settling very well at school, and they were worried because they'd put
him on a rosta system of local parents for taking him to and fro each
day. Graham confessed to a further anxiety, caused by the fact that he
wanted another child but Kath wasn't so sure.

DOMESTIC ARRANGEMENT STRESS

Most of the items on this list consisted of Kath's grumbles over the
many chores involved in running a home as well as a job, chores made

worse by Graham's role as, at best, a reluctant (and largely ineffectual) helper. Graham meanwhile objected to having to do what he called the 'messy' jobs around the house, but when pressed for details withdrew behind vague generalities about emptying dustbins and getting in the coal, and abandoned his position altogether when Kath demanded the exact dates and times when he'd actually performed any of these duties.

NEIGHBOURHOOD PRESSURES

Kath and Graham were unanimous on this one. Mortgage repayments were a major worry to them, but a more immediate concern was the amount of crime in the area. A further concern was a large extension that their neighbours were proposing to build at the rear of their property. Kath and Graham had lodged an official objection to the proposal, and were waiting for the local authority's decision. If the extension went ahead, they were convinced it would ruin their view and substantially reduce the value of their property.

MANAGING STRESS IN THE HOME

Discussing their list together, it quickly became clear that what was needed was a form of contract, with both partners agreeing to change certain of their ways to suit the other. The idea of a 'contract' seemed a little strange at first, until Kath pointed out that the marriage ceremony was itself a contract, except that it was a 'very vague and out-dated one'.

In terms of the contract they compiled together, Graham agreed to take on certain specific domestic chores (which included being exclusively responsible for tidying his own things). He also agreed to discourage his friends from calling around during certain hours of the evening and weekend which were designated 'family time'. A notepad was provided beside the telephone, and Graham promised to write all Kath's messages on it before wiping the answerphone clean. In return, Kath undertook to stop making Graham jealous at parties (a strategy which she admitted was largely a way of working off her resentment at him for his uncooperative behaviour in the house), to plan ahead more in various agreed areas, and as indicated above to leave Graham to tidy his own things.

Domestic arrangement stress was tackled at the same time as partner stress, with Kath and Graham dividing up the domestic chores more equitably, and Kath promising that she wouldn't interfere in the way in which Graham went about the tasks that fell to him. Child stress was not so easily resolved, but Kath and Graham realised they had to reassess the priority they'd been giving to Nicholas in their lives. If he was as important to them as they believed, then a way must be found for one or other of them to take and fetch him from school, or at least for him to be taken and fetched by the same neighbour each day, even if they had to pay for his or her services. The issue of whether or not to have a second child still hasn't been resolved, but enough has been said at least to let Graham realise that if a second child does come along, he must expect to make as many changes in life style as Kath to cope with it.

Neighbourhood stress was tackled firstly by more careful budgeting over the mortgage (both Kath and Graham made a list of all the regular items of expenditure they felt they could do without, and were surprised at how much money was involved), secondly by taking the initiative in forming a neighbourhood watch scheme and in asking the crime prevention officer to come and advise them on how to make their road a safer place in which to live, and thirdly by deciding exactly what they would do to *accommodate* to their neighbour's extension if it was actually built. By looking objectively at the plans and at the effect the new building would have upon them, they identified that their main objection to it was a resistance to change, rather than a realistic fear that it would spoil their outlook and devalue their property.

Not all domestic stress can be tackled as amicably and sensibly as this. But the example does show how discussing domestic problems can help in identifying their exact nature and why they are causing distress. Often even well-established partners, to say nothing of parents and children, are unaware of how deeply their behaviour is troubling other family members, and of how it is often possible to change this behaviour, especially where there is the promise that other people will respond by changing in equally helpful ways.

Chapter Six

Managing Yourself

SCHOOLING

We now come to the vital matter of what I earlier called 'schooling', that is how to train ourselves so that our cognitive appraisals stand a fair chance of affecting our responses to stressors. Making the right cognitive appraisals helps us to alter our thinking in more realistic and effective ways. And when we've looked at what it is in us that makes us an easy target, we can make decisions on where and how we need to change, and often carry these decisions through successfully. But there remains in many cases the problem of how to let our thoughts adequately influence our emotions. It's all very well to decide to *ignore or adapt to*, but how do we manage this if in spite of what our head tells us our body keeps sending out alarm signals and mustering our citizen army for fight or flight?

Which brings us back once more to our strawberry-eating friend, dangling in space and with death imminent, yet able to savour the sweetness of his strawberries to the full. Let's suppose for a moment we can enter the pages of his story book, scare away his tigers and against all the odds haul him to safety. We dust him down, and when he's finished munching his strawberries he smiles at us and thanks us for our help. Now's our chance to ask him his secret, so we grab his arm as he prepares to leave and invite him to make himself comfortable on the nearest boulder and answer a few questions. With a nod of agreement he takes his seat and looks at us expectantly. We rather wish we'd had more experience in addressing someone who may well be what is called a Zen master, and we begin rather hesitantly.

Q. *Er . . . forgive me, but I couldn't help noticing how much you* *seemed to be enjoying your strawberries.*

A. But of course. Don't you like strawberries too?

Q. *Certainly I do. But I don't think I could enjoy them if I were hanging over a cliff face a few seconds away from violent death.*

A. You should say 'possible violent death'. You see, I did not die after all.

Q. *Yes but you were only seconds away from it. If I hadn't happened to. . . .*

A. At every moment of our lives we are only seconds away from possible death. What has that got to do with whether strawberries taste sweet or not?

Q. *Yes I suppose we are. Only we don't think about it. Whereas if we were hanging over a cliff. . . .*

A. So *thought* is the enemy. You seem to be saying that although you know that throughout your life you're only seconds away from possible death, this doesn't disturb you because you don't think about it. You would need to be hanging over a cliff before the real nature of your predicament would become apparent to you.

Q. *Well yes, I suppose that **is** what I'm saying. But we can't go through life worrying all the time about sudden death. We'd never get any fun out of things.*

A. And if I'd gone through the last minutes worrying about falling from the cliff face I'd never have got any pleasure out of the strawberries.

Q. *Yes all right. I do see the point in what you're saying. Awful things could happen to us at any moment, but if we're always thinking about them we'd never be able to get on with the business of living. We'd never be able to enjoy the present moment.*

A. The present moment is all we have.

Q. *But does that mean we should never plan for the future? I'm not sure life would be possible if we always went around like that.*

A. It doesn't mean that at all. Planning for the future is very useful, ***provided*** we can be reasonably sure about that future and about the way our planning is likely to affect it. If I'd realised there were tigers in this region and a steep cliff face and mice who habitually gnaw through shrubs I would have been very foolish to take my walk in this direction. But once I'd done so, and once I'd fallen over the cliff, there was nothing I could do to save myself. Anyone could see that. So planning would have been no use at all.

Q. *But surely you must have been thinking about how hard the rocks* *were at the foot of the cliff and how sharp the tiger's teeth?*

(At this our friend laughs so heartily that he's unable to answer for a moment. Finally he wipes his eyes and his kind face becomes serious again.)

A. What would have been the use? What is the point of distressing yourself with the power of your own imagination? Certainly I meet people all the time who tell me of their worries on what might befall them. I marvel at their ingenuity, but I sorrow for their unnecessary suffering. Had I fallen from the cliff, I would soon have experienced the exact hardness of the rocks and the exact sharpness of the tiger's teeth. In the meantime, there was nothing to be gained by speculating about them.

Q. *Yes I see. Don't invent disasters for yourself before they happen. Don't waste time anticipating how a future disaster is going to feel before it actually strikes. Like futile planning, these inventions just get in the way of enjoying the present. I can see the advantages in that. But what about the past? You don't seem to be shaking. How is it you're not reliving every moment of your ghastly experience?*

A. The past is there to be learnt from. I have already learnt there are grave dangers in these regions, and I shall be careful to avoid them in the future. But now I've digested that lesson, there would be no point in going over and over the incident in my mind. It is now better to turn my mind to other things. Dwelling in the past can be as futile and as – what is the word you people use? 'stressful'? – as dwelling in the future.

(A long pause develops. Everything our friend has said is true. And yet. And yet. Does it take us very much further forward? Does it explain to us how knowing these things with our head and knowing them with our emotions can become part and parcel of the same thing?)

Q. *I'm still puzzled. It's one thing to know all this, it's quite another to* **feel** *it. However much I remind myself of all you've been saying, I've still got a nasty feeling that if I were hanging over that cliff my heart would be pounding like a drum and I'd be screaming my head off. How come you were able to stay so unaffected by it all?*

A. Because my mind turned naturally from one thing to the next, fully absorbed in what it was doing at the moment. When I saw there was nothing I could do to save myself, my mind turned from that problem to the sight of the strawberries, and from the sight of the strawberries to the taste of them.

Q. *Ah. So it sounds to me as if concentration is the answer. If you can* **concentrate** *upon what you're doing in any given moment, without distracting yourself with irrelevancies such as the things that went wrong earlier in the day or the things that might go wrong a bit later, you can enjoy the stress-free experiences as they arise.*

A. Exactly. Though I prefer the word 'awareness' to the word 'concentration'. 'Concentration' makes it sound as if you're fighting hard to do something that isn't natural. 'Awareness' (or 'mindfulness') shows that it's a natural process. Putting the mind fully into the experience of our lives, moment by moment, as we live them.

Q. *Yes I can see I'm going to have to try and do that. I've done all I can to make my life less stressful, but I still find there's something in* **me** *that needs working on. 'Putting the mind fully into the experience of our lives.' I'm not sure I'll be able to do it with my own particular cliffs and tigers, but I'll certainly try.*

(Our friend rises from his seat, smiles once more in our direction, and turns to go.)

Q. *Just one last question. If you* **had** *fallen from the cliff, what would have been going through your mind in the few seconds on the way down?*

(Our friend starts to laugh again, then stops suddenly and looks grave, as if he doubts we have understood a word he has been saying.)

A. What would have been going through my mind in the few seconds on the way down? Why nothing of course. I should have been far too busy enjoying my first experience of free fall. And now my dear friend, I think I can see some more wild strawberries over there. Let us go and enjoy them together.

YES BUT . . .

So now we know his secret. Even in the most stressful of days, there are countless events that are not stressful at all. The actual bad moments may be relatively few in number. The problem is that we can't stop hanging onto them; we let them dominate our thinking and our emotions throughout the day, to the extent that we miss opportunities to enjoy the much more frequent good moments – good moments that would quickly revive and relax us and make us much more fitted to join the fray again when the next instalment of stress arrives. Our minds cannot turn freely from one experience to the next, appreciating, as our friend might put it, the moment-by-moment business of being alive.

Another short story illustrates the point in a different way. Two monks, travelling from one monastery to another, came to a swollen river. The swirling torrent made the ford dangerous, and a young girl stood hesitantly on the bank, fearing to be swept away if she dared to attempt it. Without a word, one of the monks bent down and placed her on his shoulders, and not without difficulty gained the further bank, where he set her down and continued his journey. The second monk fell in beside him, but walked in silence, refusing to respond to his companion's attempts at conversation. However, after a while he could contain himself no longer, and burst out 'You know our vows forbid us even to look at women, and yet you actually touched that girl and carried her on your shoulders'.

'Ah' said the first monk, 'so that's what's worrying you. *I* put that girl down as soon as we'd crossed the river. *You're* still carrying her.'

The story nicely emphasises the way in which we can't put our worries (or upsets, or antagonisms, or resentments, or humiliations) down the moment they're over. Instead, we cling on to them (sometimes even perversely enjoying them!), allowing them to come between us and whatever it is we have to do next. If we prefer our illustrations from rather nearer home, top golfers demonstrate how the people who win major world tournaments are those who can leave their mistakes and their 'what-might-have-beens' behind them at the previous hole. Golfers who go on fretting over their near misses, or fuming over their opponent's good fortune, when they move from one hole to the next are at a severe disadvantage when compared to golfers who put each hole out of their minds as it is completed, and turn single-mindedly to the business of playing the one that lies ahead.

Yes but . . . if it was that easy, there would be a lot more top golfers in the world. Yes but . . . it's all very well to talk. These 'yes buts . . .' are understandable enough. They indicate the extent to which as we grow up we allow our minds to become preoccupied with thoughts, so much so that thoughts become our masters rather than our servants. They refuse to allow us to switch off one train of thinking and switch on another as the need arises. To the question 'who's in charge inside our heads?' the answer all too often has to be 'Certainly not I'.

None of this is inevitable. We aren't programmed to lose control so comprehensively of our own thought processes. The cause lies largely with our highly complex and verbal society, which demands from an early age that a massive premium be placed upon thinking, thinking, and yet more thinking. Descartes's famous dictum, 'I think therefore I am' so dominates our Western view of human nature that many of us accept unquestioningly that if we stop thinking we cease to be ourselves.

Nothing could be further from the truth. Music lovers don't cease to be themselves when they become totally absorbed in the experience of listening to music. Neither do creative people when they become caught up in the creation of their painting or their pottery or their flower arranging. In fact, they often speak of thoughts as intrusive, and as coming between them and the full expression of their creative urge. Nor (to take a contrasting example), do men and women of action cease to be themselves when fully engaged in their chosen pursuits. Racing drivers, downhill skiers, martial artists all speak of having no time to think when their minds become utterly focused upon the tasks connected with their occupations. They also testify to never feeling so fully alive as when engaged in these tasks. To imagine we're only ourselves when thinking is to take a very limited view of what it means to be human. Often it's the ability to forget that 'we' are the doers of our actions that frees us to invest fully in these actions, and to savour the full pleasure that they're able to bring. The 'we' is in any case primarily a set of concepts that we have about ourselves, and in identifying with these concepts rather than with the actual experience of doing, we risk losing much of what this experience has to offer.

One further example that I find resonates with most people: if we stand up to speak before a large gathering, or if we enter a crowded room and all eyes turn towards us, we're much more likely to be nervous and embarrassed and make a fool of ourselves if our attention is focused upon 'me' rather than upon the other people and the experiences of seeing and hearing that are being offered to us. (The very word that we use for our feelings in situations like this, *self-conscious*, is all too appropriate.) If we feel a fool we look a fool. But if we forget ourselves and turn our attention outwards, taking in the experiences of the moment, deliberately avoiding the temptation to judge them and start cerebrating about them, we free ourselves to be spontaneous and at ease, and to come across much more as 'ourselves' than can the shambling buffoon to which too much thinking about self ('How do I look? What do they think of me? Oh *hell*') all too often reduces us.

THE VALUE OF MEDITATION

If we'd been able to question our strawberry-eating friend at greater length, he would probably have told us that the ability to develop *attention*, to turn the mind easily from one thing to another, and to gain more control over our thought processes, is greatly enhanced by the practice of what is usually called *meditation*. Actually, the word is rather vague, in that sometimes it is taken to mean deliberate attempts to ponder over some concept or other. The word is actually thought to come from the Latin *meditari*, which means 'frequent', and there are also connections with the Indo-European root *med*, which denotes 'measure'. This is of limited help, though if it is to be of much use, meditation must certainly be frequent and certainly measured (in the sense of regular). Frequent and regular meditation, even if only for a few minutes each day, does four things that are vital in a stress-reducing programme.

1. It trains the attention.

2. It increases control over thought processes.

3. It increases the ability to handle emotions.

4. It aids physical relaxation.

In fact it is no exaggeration to say that, properly used, meditation is one of the most helpful psychological techniques available to us in developing the resources needed to counter stress and anxieties, worries, and negative mental and emotional states generally.

Meditation has been used, particularly in the context of spiritual development, for thousands of years. The Buddha, around 500 BC, gave careful instructions on how to meditate, and there are references in Hindu literature that go back to even earlier times. The Christian Church, particularly in its 'Eastern' branches (Russian and Greek Orthodox for example) also has its meditative traditions, but generally we in the West have neglected them in recent centuries, and are now having to relearn them, often from teachers with a Buddhist or Hindu background. There are a wide range of techniques available, but they all have a common central theme, and it is this theme upon which I shall concentrate. It lies at the heart of meditation, and is responsible for the four benefits I listed a moment ago.

This theme is *awareness*. The mind has got into the habit of flitting from one thought to another, of following first this chain of associations then that, of existing in a state of almost constant distraction while our thoughts chatter away at us like a cartload of monkeys. To handle all this, meditation bids us select a single object or experience, and stay calmly focused on it. As thoughts arise, we refuse to become diverted from our chosen object or experience. We make no attempt to push our thoughts away, or to stop them arising. We simply deny them attention. Whether the thoughts are good or bad, happy or unhappy, we let them pass into and out of the mind without holding on to them and without allowing them to set off the usual train of judgements and associations. If our mind does become distracted by a particular thought (and this happens all too often, particularly at first, providing ample proof of how much we're in need of the training that meditation brings), we coax it gently back to our point of focus the moment we realise what has happened. We don't become impatient with ourselves or give up the whole thing in disgust. We're grateful to our mind for letting us realise that it's become distracted, and we focus our attention.

The point of focus, the object or experience upon which we've chosen to meditate, can be virtually anything. Some traditions teach the use of what is called a mantra, a single word or phrase which is repeated over and over again and to which we give our full attention. Others use a mandala, a geometrical design upon which we gaze with full attention. Others teach a practice which involves visualising a symbol or a mandala, and focusing upon it with the inner eye. Others bid you to sit with open eyes before a blank white wall, and concentrate upon that. But one of the best techniques is to use your breathing.

We place our attention *either* upon the nostrils where we can feel the cool air entering as we breathe in, and the warm air exiting as we breathe out, *or* we concentrate upon the gentle rise and fall of the abdomen. In neither case do we try to follow the progress of the breath along the windpipe and into the lungs. We stay focused at just the one point of the nostrils or the abdomen, and do not allow our attention to wander from there. To help us, it is often useful, particularly in the early weeks and months of practice, to count each breath, going from one to 10 and then back again to one, over and over again. If we lose track in our counting, we go back to one and start again. Concentration develops more rapidly if we confine this counting to the out-breath, keeping silent on the in-breath, and thus demanding a little more of our powers of attention than if we count on both out- and in-breaths.

MEDITATION STEP BY STEP

Using this method, let's look step by step at how you should go about a session of meditation.

☐ Choose a time and a place when you're unlikely to be disturbed. Unplug the telephone or take it off the hook.

☐ Sit in an upright chair, or cross-legged on a firm cushion. Clasp your hands lightly in your lap. Throughout the session, keep the body upright. Do not allow the head or shoulders to sag, or the back to slump. Keeping this upright posture, relax the muscles as much as possible.

☐ Close your eyes, and allow your attention to focus gently upon the breathing. *Don't strain*. Keep everything light and calm.

☐ Allow the sensation of your breathing to occupy your full awareness. Whether you're focusing on the nostrils or on the abdomen, keep the sensation of breathing as your point of focus. Don't shift from nostrils to abdomen or vice versa. Choose one point of focus and stick with it. Don't allow your attention to follow your breath as it moves through your body. Allow it to rest consistently at the chosen place.

☐ If you're counting, count silently 'one' on the first out-breath, 'two' on the second, 'three' on the third and so on until you get to ten. When you reach ten, count backwards on each out-breath until you get to one. Then back up again to ten, and so on. If you lose track of your counting at any point, go back to one and start again.

☐ When thoughts arise, neither follow them nor try to push them away. Don't label them as 'good' or 'bad', whatever they contain. Simply keep your attention on your breathing and not upon your thoughts. Allow them to pass into and out of the mind without attending to them or hindering them.

☐ When the meditation session is over, rise slowly from your seat. Try to maintain something of the poised awareness experienced (however briefly) in meditation as you go about your business. Try to be aware of the sights and sounds around you in the same way you were aware of your breathing; without rushing to conceptualise about them or to pass judgements or to set off trains of associations.

To begin with, it doesn't really matter how long you sit in meditation each session. Don't set yourself impossible targets. You won't stick to them, and you'll quickly become discouraged. Regular, daily practice, at the same time each day, is far more important than how long you sit. Five minutes a day is often ample for a beginner, and as the days go by the time will often lengthen of its own accord. Eventually you may be sitting for 15 or 20 minutes a day or more, but it will seem much less.

As to time of day, some people prefer first thing in the morning, others last thing at night. And a few people other times during the day. Keeping to a set time is more important than when that time happens to be. And once your practice of meditation becomes an established part of your life, you'll find that in addition to your set times you can turn your attention to your breathing and feel yourself calming down whenever the day becomes stressful or whenever you find you want to do so. For although meditation requires a set time and a set place and a set posture if you're to train yourself properly in the technique, you don't have to confine it *only* to those times. Out walking, sitting in the office, riding in a train, you can turn your awareness away from the chatter of your thoughts and towards your breathing. Don't be afraid that doing this will send you off into a world of your own, inattentive to what is happening around you. Meditation is simply the practice of awareness, and if you're meditating out in the open you can turn this awareness, once it's established, away from your breathing and towards the things surrounding you. Most of the time when out walking, for example, we don't really *see* anything properly, because our minds are so preoccupied with our internal monologue that we haven't the time to look about us and take things in. How often, for example, do you find yourself stumped when asked for directions to a street quite near your home? You must have passed it hundreds of times, but you've never once allowed its name to register on your awareness. And how familiar (and how stressful!) is the experience that 'I had it in my hands not a moment ago; now *where* did I put it?'. The reason it's so infuriatingly hard to remember is that your awareness was somewhere else when you put the object, whatever it was, down. Instead of focusing on the action of the moment, you were lost inside your own head or allowing your attention to be pulled in all directions by trying to do umpteen things at once.

Many people discover that when they first start the practice of meditation, all goes well for a few days. They find themselves much calmer and more peaceful, and go around loudly extolling its virtues. A few days further on still, and things begin to go sour. They find they can't concentrate very well after all. Or that other, more pressing things keep cropping up which prevent them sparing the time for it. What's happened is that the novelty has worn off. Our minds crave variety, and instead of realising that meditation is specifically about dealing with this craving, so that the mind can stay calmly focused, many novices succumb to it at the very time when their meditation is about to do them some real good. It's vital to keep up our practice during this early flat period, until the meditation begins to establish itself properly and we start finding the benefits in our daily lives.

So the moral is, decide on a time of day when you can practice meditation for a few minutes, and keep at it. The next hazard to watch for is the temptation to give up when you're going through a particularly stressful period. People tend to say 'I can meditate okay when my life is peaceful, but when things get really hectic at work, my mind is so chaotic that I just can't focus on my breathing for ten seconds together. So there's no point in trying to practice'. The answer is that these are just the times when the practice is of most importance. It's at these times that we most need the discipline of turning our awareness away from our thinking, and it's at these times that we actually learn most about how to do so. So however you feel, go to your meditation chair or cushion at the usual time and sit on it. Close your eyes, focus on your breathing, and begin.

MEDITATION AND EMOTIONS

Now we come to the point where meditation helps us with our emotions. Through dealing with our thoughts instead of letting them always deal with us, we become calmer, more peaceful. The links between getting it right in the head and getting it right in the body begin to be made. But we can also use meditation specifically for working on the emotions. Having sat for a few minutes and focused upon our breathing, we can deliberately allow into our awareness the memory of some angry or hurtful experience we had during the day. Usually the memory of this experience would bring an immediate emotional reaction. But now, in the tranquility of meditation, the memory comes back to us without any emotional jolt. We look at it with the detachment we've learnt to show towards any thoughts that arise during meditation, and the peaceful state of the body does the rest. Instead of arousal, we experience equanimity, and this equanimity begins to defuse the memory even when it returns at other times. It also allows us to be more honest about the emotion, and to identify those occasions when in fact we've clung to it through the perverse 'enjoyment' of having a grudge or a feeling of being ill-used.

If however, at this time or any other, strong emotions do arise in meditation, this is a welcome opportunity to look at them with just that little bit more objectivity than we can usually manage. Instead of automatically identifying with them, the practice is to observe them, without attaching any particular importance to them. We can stare into them, so to speak, and analyse them into their constituent parts. What is this strange thing called 'fear' or 'anger' or 'resentment' or 'embarrassment' that usually overwhelms me? Where is it? Can I locate it somewhere in my body? In my mind? Can I see where it comes from and where it goes? If I usually think of it as unpleasant, where and what is this unpleasantness?

After a few moments of this analysis, we realise that the emotion is very much less substantial than we'd always imagined. It may be little more than a tingling sensation, or a hot sensation, or a churning sensation. That's all. Not only does this help the emotion to lose some of its mystery and its power over us, it also allows it to fade away under our gaze. It isn't something real and hard and objective 'out there'. It's something nebulous and shifting and changing 'in here'. The longer we look at it, the more insubstantial it becomes, and the more we grasp the fact that it just isn't true to say that other people 'make' us afraid or angry or upset. We do it to ourselves. There are no magic buttons for them to come up and press. The emotion is something for which, ultimately, we ourselves are responsible.

MEDITATION AND PHYSICAL RELAXATION

In the same way that we can deliberately switch our awareness in meditation from our breathing to our emotions (the accent here is upon 'deliberately'; in meditation we consciously make the decisions, instead of allowing the mind to wander at will), so we can switch it to our body. The idea is to sweep the body gently, and identify all the pockets of physical tension that build up during the day, and then calmly let the tension go. Focus first on the eyes. Are they unnecessarily screwed shut, instead of simply closed? Then let the attention sweep slowly (rather than leap jerkily) to the forehead, then the scalp, then the back of the neck, then the back itself, then down the arms and the hands, then back up to the jaw and down the chest and the abdomen. And so on down to the feet. There's no hurry. Nothing in meditation should ever be allowed to feel hard or difficult or competitive. Time isn't important. We aren't trying to win a race. Allow the awareness to flow, and each time it comes upon a little knot of tension, or even upon a muscle which is just that little bit more stressed than it need be to hold us in our upright position, we let the tension go. If you're physically very tense, do the exercise every time you meditate. Become aware if the tension creeps back into the muscles almost as soon as you've dealt with it, and when this happens, let it go once more.

Not only does this exercise make you generally more relaxed, it also increases body awareness. So when you're at work you become much more aware of the moments when groups of muscles start to tense up. Once tensed, they have a habit of remaining tense throughout the day. But with body awareness, we can let that tension go each time it arises. So the backache, the bellyache, the tension headache, the tight jaw, the stiff neck and shoulders, the strained eyes, the tense and worried frown, don't have a chance to develop. Not only do we feel much better, but the emotional and physical energy that went into maintaining these knots of tension is saved for more useful purposes, and we end the day surprised at how much less tired we feel, and how much readier we are to pursue a hobby or a leisure interest when we get home in the evening, instead of spending the time slumped in front of the television.

MEDITATION AND MINDFULNESS

I've said that as we train our awareness (or become more *mindful*) we notice things around us much more clearly, and don't so frequently have that experience of putting something down and then immediately having no earthly idea of where we put it. But we can assist this process with another exercise, closely linked to meditation. Since it is very difficult to stay mindful for any length of time once we've come out of meditation, the exercise involves occupying our thoughts with simple descriptions (a kind of running commentary) of what it is we're actually doing at this moment. I said in Chapter 3 that one frequently reported cause of stress is having to do more than one thing at a time. We're trying to compose a letter, the phone rings; while we're answering it someone comes in the room and puts some papers on our desk marked 'urgent'; we squint at them while we're talking, and notice next to them on the desk another pile of papers we were in the middle of filing when we had to stop in order to compose the letter; and so on. No wonder that after a few minutes of this we have no recollection of what it was we were just doing, or where we had just put things down. If however we prompt ourselves to notice what we're doing at the moment when we do it, things become much clearer and we become much less harassed.

We need to say to ourselves, in the form of a sub-vocal running commentary, 'OK, I'm in the middle of filing and I've remembered that important letter I need to compose. So I'm putting the papers for filing down on the desk here, and turning to the letter. Now I'm turning from the letter to answer the phone. Now I'm noticing some papers being dumped on my desk; I'll look at them after I come off the telephone'. And so on. Sounds strange? So does letting ourselves be run ragged by one hundred and one things competing for our attention at every moment. And if we were able to practise mindfulness naturally we wouldn't need an internal commentary like this. But it does work. The mind becomes calmer, more deliberate, more able to choose which things to attend to, instead of being pulled and pushed helplessly by events. And almost miraculously, we can remember now where it was we put down those important papers when the telephone rang, or who it was we were on our way to see when we were waylaid in the corridor, or what it was we were planning to do when an unexpected visitor arrived. We end up being more efficient, less frayed at the edges, and with the confidence-boosting feeling that *we're* in charge of events.

The only way to find if meditation helps you in your own stress-reduction programme is to try it. If you say you want some proof before you're prepared to invest any of your time in it, talk to experienced meditators and observe their behaviour. Do they seem to have anything about them that you'd rather like for yourself? Do they seem to handle stress better? To be that bit more tranquil and happy, that bit more efficient in their work, that bit more open to the joys of life? If the answer is yes, then this is the kind of proof you need. Use it to help you get started, and then look for further proof in the effect that your practice is having upon your own state of being.

OTHER FORMS OF RELAXATION

As should be apparent, meditation doesn't involve relaxing into a sleepy, trance-like state. But relaxation is important, so in addition to meditation, it is worth cultivating the art of relaxation for its own sake. In relaxation, the mind and body are released from conscious demands, and become free of tensions. This is not as easy as it sounds. Many people claim despairingly that they just can't relax (or 'unwind'), and spend most of their waking lives taut as a watch spring. The reasons are firstly that their minds are never still, and secondly that they have insufficient body awareness to spot those moments during the day when they begin to tense up. This is one reason why meditation and relaxation, though separate practices, go so easily together. Meditators can usually relax with no difficulty, because their medi-

─── WATER – INSIDE AND OUT ───

The physiological effects of stress include dehydration and consequent thickening of the blood, under-nourishment of the skin, digestive disorders, and general upsets in metabolism (see pages 7–9). An important countermeasure to dehydration is to increase your intake of liquid.

Tea, coffee and alcohol are diuretics (they actually *increase* the rate at which liquid is lost) so they're no help. Instead, go for pure water, or for natural unsweetened fruit juices. Experts suggest that when under stress you should drink around four pints of suitable liquid every day, in addition to the liquid you get from food and from milk on cereals and in beverages. This means eight glasses of water.

If you think this is going to be difficult, console yourself with the thought of how much better you're going to look. The body is nine tenths water, and some of the visible effects of ageing are simply dehydration. We don't drink enough water, even when we aren't stressed, to keep ourselves looking and feeling in full health.

Water has a toning effect outside the body as well as inside. A shower helps to relieve stress partly because the droplets enhance the negative ions in the air you breathe. But the feel of water on the skin has a soothing effect in itself. We all know the luxury of a long soak in a hot bath at the end of the day. But a cold shower is, except last thing at night, even better. (I have been extolling the value of cold showers to family and friends for years, though without conspicuous success.)

tation has trained them in calming the mind and in sensitivity to bodily sensations.

There are many books available on relaxation techniques, and some of them are very good. But their effectiveness is limited by the fact that they tend to treat relaxation as something distinct from everyday life. You go into a quiet room, lie down and run through your relaxation routine. The trouble is that even if the routine goes well, five minutes after you've finished it and rejoined the world you're as tense as ever once again. Relaxation is only really of value if it goes hand-in-hand with enhanced body awareness, so that throughout the day you're easily and pleasantly in harmony with your body, conscious the moment muscles are tensing up or the rhythm of the breathing is interrupted, and able at once to unclench yourself and restore the body to its natural unstressed state.

As you become more aware of your body, so you realise that tension arises as a way of gearing the body for action. In itself, tension is natural, but the energy behind it should be discharged in this action, and the body allowed immediately afterwards to relax again. The tension is simply part of the mobilisation of the citizen army (fight or flight), and as soon as the emergency passes, the army stands down and the tension disappears. The problem arises of course, as with all aspects of the physiological response to stress, when the environment doesn't allow us to discharge our mobilised energy, and the tension remains in our muscles (and in the narrowing of our blood vessels), until by the end of the day they're bunched like those of a prize fighter about to step into the boxing ring.

The solution is to release the tension the moment it arises. When you feel muscles knot themselves ready for action, you instruct them that the action isn't necessary, and that they can open and release the tension. The process is a conscious one at first (though it takes only a moment's awareness each time), but soon becomes semi-automatic, and as the practice develops, so the body gets the message that the tension usually isn't necessary in the first place, and a relaxed state becomes more and more habitual.

The same procedure applies to our breathing. When we're geared up for an emergency, there's often a tendency to hold our breath (notice how natural a reaction this is for example when we bend down to lift a heavy weight). A similar thing can happen when we're in a stressful conversation with someone, or even in a pleasant but animated one. What happens is we take in a gulp of air ready to have our say, we get interrupted, and clamp down on the breath and hold it, either momentarily or until we can get a word in edgeways. The upshot of all this is that our breathing pattern becomes very disrupted and irregular. With increased body awareness we become conscious of this the moment it happens, and immediately allow the breathing to relax back into its usual rhythm.

So relaxation is very much a matter for the whole of our waking life, not just for those moments when we're able to flop onto the settee at home. Start your relaxation programme therefore by getting to know, from the inside, the feel of your own body. If you're meditating, you will already be doing this through the sweeping technique described on p. 93. If you're not, practise the following routine regularly, daily if possible. It takes only a few minutes of your time.

RELAXATION PROGRAMME 1

☐ Choose a quiet room and a time when you're unlikely to be disturbed.

☐ Wear nothing or very light clothing.

☐ Lie on your back on the floor or a firm surface.

☐ Tense the muscles in your right foot and ankle. Wriggle your toes. How does it feel? Clench the muscles and release them several times. Notice the difference in sensation between the clenched and unclenched muscles. Commit it to memory.

☐ Repeat the exercise with your left foot and ankle.

☐ Tense the calf muslces, first one then the other. Repeat several times, alternately clenching and unclenching. Once again notice the difference in sensation between the tense and the relaxed state. Remember it.

☐ Move next to the thigh muscles, and carry out the same exercise. Notice how tension in the thighs affects the kneecaps and the knees.

☐ Now move to the muscles of the buttocks and anus (a favourite site of unnecessary tension). Notice once more the difference in sensation between tension and relaxation.

☐ Work upwards, taking in the muscles of the abdomen, of the chest, and of the back and shoulders, working upon each group in turn.

☐ Now work on the biceps, the forearms and the hands.

☐ Lastly, move to the neck, the jaw, the face and forehead, and the scalp.

You may find that some groups of muscles just don't seem to relax, however hard you try. Don't become discouraged. Be patient with yourself. You can't undo the bad habits of years in five minutes. Don't try too hard, this only increases the tension. Spend just a few moments on those muscles each day, until gradually they come under your proper control. Movement often helps. So if it's the jaw that won't relax, waggle it from side to side before trying to relax it. If it's the hands, flex and unflex the fingers. If it's the arms, press them hard against the floor and then release them. If it's the abdomen, try one or two sit-ups (no more unless you're fit – the stomach muscles can easily be strained). If it's the legs, bicycle in the air for a moment. And so on.

Supplement this programme by running through a similar routine when you're at work. Notice how when sitting at a desk you're slumping and having to tense certain muscles in order to hold the position. Notice how your body is thrown out of balance when you sit in a chair and cross one leg over the other. Notice the unnecessary strain you put into carrying out simple tasks, like climbing stairs, opening drawers, picking up objects. Notice how you tighten your face muscles with quite unnecessary effort when you're doing even the simplest things (washing dishes, putting on your coat, eating your food). Notice how you frown, how you tense your eye muscles, how you clench your teeth. Begin to enjoy your body more, and the sheer pleasure of moving it without tension and strain, and of sinking into relaxed stillness. Notice how much nicer it is to do things smoothly and not jerkily, how peaceful you feel when you stop nervously twitching or fiddling with objects or restlessly pacing about. Stand in front of a full-length bedroom mirror (naked if you can face the sight) and look at yourself from all angles. See how tension has affected your posture. Is one shoulder higher than the other? Are your shoulders hunched and your head and neck thrust forward, as if braced for action that never comes? Are your knees locked tight instead of being relaxed and very slightly bent? Do the muscles of your back and buttocks scream tension at you? Does your spine look out of alignment? Is your lower back hollowed with strain, instead of straight and poised? From the side, are your ears, hands and knees in a straight line, or is your neck thrust so far forward and your back so curved that you look like a capital letter 'S'?

If you're still game after all this, pile some pillows or cushions on the floor, and just collapse onto them. Are you able to go down like a sack of potatoes, letting gravity do the work for you? Or is there resistance from tense muscles? Repeat the exercise several times. If the pillows and cushions are soft enough, you ought to be able to drop straight down. If you don't like the analogy of a sack of potatoes, think of a marionette when the puppeteer releases its strings. Can you fall with the same immediacy and freedom? If not, check why. What muscles are holding you back? Or is it your mind that just won't let go? Whatever it is, trace it then release it. You may not be able to trace and release at first, but try every day until you can. This is a marvellous exercise for checking the progress you're making in relaxation. Keep at it!

RELAXATION PROGRAMME 2

The other component of your relaxation routine is to work on calming the mind. Meditation will already be doing this for you, but you can supplement it with the following exercise, which calls on the enormous potential of creative visualisation.

▶ Choose a quiet room and a time when you're unlikely to be disturbed.

▶ Lie on your back on a firm or soft surface, whichever you prefer.

▶ Close your eyes and sweep your awareness around the body, relaxing any groups of muscles that are tense.

▶ Visualise a scene you know very well. Your garden perhaps, or the front of your house. Choose a pleasant scene that has happy associations. If you can't visualise clearly, don't worry. Just work with whatever you can get. Visualisation improves with practice.

▶ Once you've established your visualisation, look closely at it for details. If it's your garden, pick out the exact position of the flower tubs, of the rose bushes, of the apple tree. Look at the colours and the shapes. Try to get them as accurately as you can, but again don't worry if they don't become very clear, or if the visualisation tends to slip away.

▶ Now dissolve the visualisation (i.e. let it go) and replace it with an imaginary scene. Choose a beach, with the calm sea sparkling in the sun, and the smooth curve of a sandy shore. Or choose a river, winding between overhanging trees, with dappled patterns of light and shade on the water. Or choose something completely different, something which appeals to you, and which is calm and full of peace.

▶ When the visualisation is as clear as you are likely to get it, imagine yourself to grow lighter and lighter . . . lighter and lighter . . . until you're drifting up off the place where you're lying, and drifting into the peaceful scene you're visualising, so that it is now all around you, and you have become part of it. Feel the *physical* sensations associated with it. The warmth of the sun upon your face, the cool water, the softness of the breeze, the sand underneath you, or the leaves brushing against your hand.

▶ As you become part of the scene, become part also of the peace within it. There is nowhere to go, nothing to do, no demands to be met, no pressures, no deadlines. Just the sensation of being at one with the peace around and within you.

▶ Stay in this state for as long as you wish, then gradually let yourself sink back onto the floor or the bed on which you're lying, and let the scene in front of you dissolve gently. Don't come back to earth too abruptly. Lie for a moment looking at the blank space left by the dissolved scene. The blue of an empty, cloudless sky, or the serenity of a smooth white screen. Then gently, when you're ready, open your eyes and come back into the present.

When the exercise is over, don't jump up and immediately put yourself back into a state of readiness for any emergency. Bring the peace back with you into your movements and your thinking. Move gently, allowing each movement to flow into the next, with a harmony between them, so that the body is working as a single unit instead of as a collection of separate parts. Keep the mind peaceful and open, not dominated by an immediate inrush of thoughts. Think relaxation, and let that relaxation spread into whatever you find yourself now having to do. Don't be disappointed or impatient if this seems impossible at first. Don't blame yourself or the exercises. Don't try too hard. It's often the very feeling that we have to put so much *effort* into things that gets in the way of doing them. But don't give up. Keep practising. Even if the peaceful state of mind and body only lasts for a few moments once you resume everyday living, this is good progress. It shows you

DIET

People under stress tend to over or undereat, or to slip into the habit of rushed, inadequate meals. Under stress, the body uses up energy much more quickly than usual, and a healthy diet becomes doubly important. In addition, the extra strain placed upon the cardiovascular system means that your heart needs all the help it can get from a 'heart-saver diet'. This is a diet that, even when we aren't over-stressed, is recommended by nutritionists as beneficial in lowering the risk of heart disease. The main principles behind the diet are:

* Cut down the intake of fat. Adults should eat no more than 80 gms of fat per day. (The amount quickly adds up when you realise how much fat goes into fried foods, pastries, ice-cream, cheese, and many processed foods. Red meat contains more fat than white meat.) Some experts consider even 80 gms is too high, and that 60 gms is nearer the mark.

* Take as much of this fat as possible in polyunsaturated rather than saturated form. Vegetable oils and some fish oils are mostly unsaturated, while red meat, hard cheese, cream, eggs and butter are mostly saturated. But frying converts polyunsaturates into saturates. So does the manufacturing process of cheap margarines and many convenience foods.

* Eat as much fresh fruit and vegetables as possible, raw if you can. When you cook, steam rather than boil. If you must boil, do it lightly.

* Eat as much fibre as possible, in the form of wholemeal bread, fibre-rich breakfast cereals, the skin of fruits and vegetables.

* Cut down on both sugar and salt. Use them only sparingly in cooking, and never add them to food at the table. Buy unsweetened tinned fruit rather than sweetened. Check labels and avoid products with added sugar and salt whenever you can.

* Cook your own food rather than eat out or buy convenience foods.

* Stress deplenishes Vitamin B. Take a good Vitamin B supplement containing all the vitamins in the B range.

* WATCH YOUR WEIGHT. Studies of agrarian communities with better diets than ours show that far from gaining weight we should actually *lose* a little weight from middle age onwards if we're to stay fit.

that peaceful states are possible. With continued practice they will become more and more a part of you.

LETTING GO OF EMOTIONS

In addition to working with emotions through meditation, some people have a strong need for other strategies for helping them contact and express their emotional life. People differ temperamentally in the strength of their various emotions, but there's general agreement (at least amongst psychologists influenced by psychoanalytical and humanistic ideas) that consistent repression of the emotions leads to psychological problems, particularly if that repression is of a blanket kind (all emotions repressed at all times) rather than of a selective kind (certain emotions repressed in certain circumstances). These psychological problems include such things as inner conflicts, depression, obsessionality, self-rejection and vague, free-floating anxiety.

There's also agreement amongst doctors interested in psychosomatic illness and mind–body links that repression of emotions can be a factor in the development of certain diseases, including some forms of cancer and heart disease. All this suggests that there are good arguments for taking the lid off your emotional life, and at least recognising that the emotions are there, even if you still feel you can't express them in public.

The essential first step is to *give yourself permission* to experience emotions. To give yourself permission to be angry, or afraid, or joyful or whatever. Much repression comes from early conditioning during which children are led to associate their emotions with something unpleasant or even downright sinful. Punished for expressing emotions, they grow into adults who just can't allow themselves to speak their minds or to boil over or to have a good time. Inhibitions have been so strongly conditioned, that they have become rigid and habitual.

So give yourself permission to have an emotional life and proper access to it. If you can't award this permission in public, award it in private. After a bad day at work, go somewhere on your own and leap up and down like an angry child and tell the boss you *won't* do as you're asked. Add a few choice observations about his or her character too if you like. On the other hand, after a good day, spring up and down in joy. Do the things a happy *child* would do. Children express their emotions in physical movement. Skipping, dancing, lying on the floor and kicking. If you never had a chance to do any of these things without adult disapproval, do them now. If you feel self-conscious about them, even when there's no one around to see or hear, ask yourself why? Why are you self-conscious even in front of yourself? The answer is usually that there's an internalised parent watching you and scolding. Face and banish the internal parent. It's only a habitual way of feeling and thinking, brought about in you by all that early conditioning. Jeer at it if you like. Tell it you're going to do as *you* want, and if that involves a tantrum or singing and dancing, then so be it.

If you want to cry, do that too. Many men have lost the gift of tears. So strong is their conditioning from boyhood upwards that they switch off the crying mechanism the moment it's activated. They would do well to remember that studies show crying alters the body's chemistry in desirable ways, reversing some of the harmful physiological stress reactions described in Chapter 1. There's even a suggestion that the lower incidence of early heart disease in women is linked in part to their ability to break down and weep when they feel the need. Due to the prejudice of others, it may not be appropriate for you to cry in public, but in private, or in the company of those you love and trust, tears release emotions and help you to acknowledge your real feelings more surely than almost any other piece of behaviour. They also help those you love and trust to understand *you* more fully, and to give you the sympathy and support that is your right when you're distressed.

By the same token, it helps you to be more open with your own emotions if you're sensitive towards emotions in others. Many people who can't release their own emotions are thrown off balance by emotion in those around them. If we can't face our own tears, we're likely to be impatient with tears in others. If we can't face our anger, we're likely to be upset by anger in others. If we can't face our fear, we're likely to be unsympathetic to fear in others. If we can't face our joy, we're likely to be embarrassed by joy in others. If we can't face our feelings of affection, we're likely to be cold towards expressions of affection in others. If we can't face our own weakness, we're likely to be tough-minded towards weakness in others.

Part of the key lies in accepting that emotions are a normal, natural, desirable, and often productive part of life. Certainly we need to be able to control them and to know when it is appropriate to express them and when it isn't. But this knowledge can only come from a clear understanding and openness towards our own emotionality. Anything less, and the stress in our lives will go on taking its physical and psychological toll.

PHYSICAL EXERCISE

Physical exercise has an important part to play in reducing the effects of stress. This makes sense when we remember once again that these effects are simply the result of the body gearing itself up for energetic action. When action isn't permitted to take place, the energy remains pent-up in the body, causing tensions and all the other unwanted physical effects. Physical exercise helps to discharge this energy, and also helps the mind turn to other things and so forget the frustrations and pressures that geared the body up in the first place. For some people, explosive, competitive sport works best, often because their tensions may be the result of anger directed towards others (boss, colleagues) which they weren't able to express. For some people, rhythmical exercises like jogging or walking or dancing are preferable, perhaps because the rhythmical movement has a calming effect. For others, the exact form of the exercise is less important than the fact that it takes them out of doors or into the company of friends.

There's good evidence that people who take regular physical exercise have more energy, feel better, and are less susceptible to stress-related diseases such as heart attacks and strokes. To become technical for a moment, regular exercise at a certain level of intensity appears to improve cardiovascular efficiency (the heart can pump more blood with each beat), to reduce blood pressure and blood sugar levels, and to improve the balance of blood lipids (specifically, blood cholesterol in the form of low density lipoprotein is lowered, while high density lipoprotein levels are raised). Exercise also raises the levels of endorphins (proteins with a similar chemical structure to opium or morphine) in the blood, and this is thought by some authorities to be responsible for the feelings of well-being that exercise often brings. It releases tension in the muscles, dilates the blood vessels, and may retard the furring up of the arteries (atheroma) which is a major factor in heart attacks. Finally, in addition to helping keep weight down, exercise helps maintain flexibility in the joints, warding off the stiffness that often accompanies tension and strain.

How much exercise is needed to produce these desirable results?

1. You can't store the beneficial effects of exercise for any length of time. Men and women who have been very athletic in their youth have no greater resistance to disease and no greater life expectancy than anyone else if they become inactive as they grow older. Therefore exercise needs to be *regular*.

2. Initially, exercise every day if possible. Once a desired level of

fitness has been reached, three times a week is considered sufficient to maintain this level.

3. Each exercise session should last a minimum of 20 minutes.
Shorter periods don't allow the body to produce the desirable
changes that constitute fitness.

4. During the exercise session, your heart rate must be raised to a
certain level if benefits are to occur. This level varies with age. The
simplest way of calculating it is to subtract your age from 190. This
gives the *upper limit* beyond which your heart should not be
allowed to go. Then subtract another 20. This gives you the *lower
limit* beneath which there will be little effect upon fitness. When
starting an exercise programme, *keep at or near the lower limit*. As
your fitness increases over the weeks, you can gradually push
yourself towards your upper limit. Don't overdo it. Exercise
should never take you beyond the point where you feel able to
hold a conversation with someone while you're doing it.

5. Above a certain level of fitness, the beneficial effects of exercise
upon your coronary risk factor fall off sharply. Twenty minutes
each day until you can work comfortably at the upper pulse limit
for your age, followed by twenty minutes three times a week to
keep you at this limit, is just as helpful (perhaps more so) than
much longer and more intensive stints. Running 20 miles a week
for example is every bit as good for you as running 100, unless
you want to be a champion athlete.

   In stress reduction terms, you can of course keep going longer
than 20 minutes if you feel comfortable and want to do so, though
there is some evidence that we can become addicted to the
endorphins released into the blood stream by over-exercising (the
so-called 'runner's high').

6. Rotating each joint once a day through its full range of flexibility is
enough to keep you supple. The old adage of 'use it or lose it' is an
excellent one when applied to joint mobility.

It goes without saying that if you have been rather inactive, you should
first check with your doctor before starting any exercise programme.
Always check if you're over 35 or have any reason to think you're badly
out of condition. It also goes without saying that the body should never
be pushed too hard. Exercise involves effort, but it doesn't have to be
painful in order to do you good. Pushing yourself too hard not only
could be dangerous, it is for most people a guaranteed way of ensuring

WHAT KIND OF EXERCISE?

The answer is whatever kind takes your pulse rate into the limits defined on page 107, and which you enjoy enough to perform every day. Most people are much more inclined to sustain an exercise programme if they undertake it socially or competitively with family or friends. You need two kinds of exercise, one to strengthen the cardiovascular system (such as jogging or cycling), and one to keep you supple and flexible (such as yoga or t'ai chi). A well-designed aerobics programme includes both, but isn't to everyone's taste.

Any kind of exercise carries dangers if you go at it too vigorously too soon, and if it drives your pulse rate up beyond the defined limits. Squash is much too vigorous if you haven't been on a suitable preliminary fitness programme, and even at the best of times squash keeps you fit *but not fit enough for playing squash*. You need a sustained, vigorous exercise programme in addition if your body is to meet the violent demands squash makes upon it. Even jogging can be dangerous if you push yourself too hard, and the jarring of the limbs caused by running on pavements can sometimes lead to knee, tendon, shin and calf muscle problems. Cycling avoids these problems, but can come up against traffic hazards. Swimming is safe if you're in a properly supervised pool, and has the additional benefit of the envigorating effect of water (see page 97). It is also better for flexibility than jogging or cycling.

The best combination is a programme of *flexibility* exercises (5 minutes per day) plus a programme of *stamina* exercises (20 minutes a day).

☐ The aim of a good flexibility programme is to flex or rotate each joint through its full range of movement at least once each session. This is best done as part of a supervised programme, but if you're working on your own, *don't force it*. Find what in yoga and t'ai chi is called your 'soft limit', and work only up to that limit. Increased flexibility and suppleness will come with time.

☐ For stamina, find something which you can do easily and in all weathers. An exercise bicycle or a rowing machine are ideal. So is a good skipping rope, and an open space in which to skip.

But whatever activity you choose, buy an electronic pulse counter that clips to your body and gives a read-out on your pulse rate, or alternatively take your pulse at regular intervals. Keep at your lower limit until fitness is established, and at all times don't exceed the upper limit. If at any time you experience chest pains or distress of any kind, *stop and check with your doctor*. And if you're over 35 or have any reason to doubt you're in good health, *check with him or her before you start the exercise programme* in the first place.

you won't keep up your exercise programme. Once your initial enthusiasm wears off, the sheer hard grind will soon lose any attraction, and things will peter out. Select an exercise you enjoy and keep the experience a pleasant one. That way the mind won't build up a resistance to doing it. But remember that *some* commitment and self-discipline are essential. As with meditation, the mind will very quickly find reasons why you shouldn't be doing it ('It's boring', 'I can't see any results', 'I haven't the time', 'I'll do it tomorrow'). Don't let the mind have everything its own way. There's no short cut to fitness. Whenever you feel like giving up your exercise programme, ask yourself 'What price *is* good health?'. If the answer comes back that it isn't worth 20 minutes a day, you have some hard thinking to do about the priorities in your life.

PERSONAL RELATIONSHIPS

Stress in your professional life is made much worse if there's stress in your domestic and social life too. Stress of this kind can stem from a number of different sources, such as those mentioned in Chapter 5 when the difficulties facing Kath and Graham were examined. Conversely, a happy domestic life, with close and loving relationships with a partner and/or with children, can have a major effect on our ability to resist stress. To be loved and needed and thought well of by our family and friends helps to restore a self-image battered by the events of the day, and allows us to enjoy a relaxing and secure base to our lives. It also reassures us that other people identify with us and care about our problems, that fundamentally we aren't isolated and do have other people on our side!

SOMEONE TO TALK TO

Great emphasis is laid by some commentators upon the need to communicate our problems to those close to us or even to sympathetic strangers in order to cope successfully with stress. And there's no doubt that if you feel the *need* to communicate, then it's important to be able to put problems into words and important to have someone around prepared to listen (and to offer sympathy and advice). But individuals vary, and some people feel much better if they can leave work behind them at the end of the day, and go home and forget about it. The last thing they want is to have someone at home just waiting to ply them with questions on how the day went. Yet others, while taking their problems home, prefer to have a period of peace and quiet when they enjoy their own company and think through and come to terms with their working day on their own. Each of these responses, provided it works for the individual, is equally valid. Some people are made to believe they're not in touch with their feelings if they don't want to rush off and lay them bare before partner or friends. Others are made to believe they're immature because they can't keep feelings to themselves. But the truth of the matter is that being in touch with one's feelings *and* maturity are best evidenced in people who have the insight into their own emtional needs and the best way to cope with them. As mentioned earlier, there is some evidence that extroverts seek company when emotionally aroused or troubled, while introverts seek solitude. Neither of these reactions can be described as 'better' than the other. Different temperaments require different strategies. Provided the *individual* is at ease with these strategies (and is also sensitive to the needs of partner and friends, who may prefer to be told things or prefer not to be burdened by them), then it's inaccurate to argue that there is a norm with which every one must comply.

DISPLACED AGGRESSION

Another important social factor is the tendency most of us have to unload the frustrations and anger and irritations that we have acquired but been unable to express at work upon the most convenient target the moment we get home. Or the tendency to refuse the perfectly reasonable requests of partner or children because we're too exhausted by the events of the day to bother with them. This can damage family life, and ultimately lead to an increase in the demands (and a decrease in the sympathy) extended to us. Hardly the best way to ease the burden of stress.

One simple expedient to help avoid displaced aggression is to be more prepared for it. Many people confess to being so preoccupied with their day at work that when they arrive home their thoughts are still very much elsewhere. So the bickering between their children or the inconvenient behaviour of their partner invariably take them by surprise. Instead of seeing the one as the natural behaviour of young-sters and the other as the perfectly legitimate self-determination of a mature adult, they feel immediately irritated or affronted and this proves to be the final straw. If instead they worked more effectively at reorientating themselves from the professional events of the day to the domestic events of the home, they'd be very much better able to cope. The reorientation should start the moment the working day is over, and continue during the journey home, so that by the time we arrive we're already in a more suitable frame of mind. This requires effort of course. It's often easier to let the mind chew over the events of the day, no matter how repetitively and unproductively. And to nurse our outrage at colleagues or bosses or clients. But this exacts an unwelcome price in terms of the domestic stress it causes. The skills practised in meditation make us more able to turn the mind from these thoughts to calmer and more home-orientated ones. But even without meditation, if we really *want* to become proficient at switching our thoughts from work to home, then with experience we can develop the necessary skills.

REAPPRAISING YOUR LIFE

It's very easy to become so immersed in our stress that we can't afford the time or personal space to stand back and reappraise our objectives in life and our methods for achieving them. Yet such periodic appraisal is vital. Are we in the right job after all? Is it taking us where we want to go? Have we the right qualities for making a success of it? Are we relating as we should to colleagues, clients and family? Are our priorities right? Are we making space for our own interests, for some leisure time? Do we place relaxation and just doing nothing – just *being* – high enough on our list? (It was Maslow, the founder of humanistic psychology, who deplored the fact that psychology textbooks never have chapters on what he called 'loafing about', that vital occupation that gives us time for just being who we are instead of who we think we are, or who we want to be, or who other people think we are.)

As children, many professional people were taught always to think ahead, to develop ambitions and the qualifications necessary to achieve them, to defer present satisfactions in the interests of long-term goals. This is a valuable training, but it goes wrong when it is emphasised at the expense of *also* relaxing and taking pleasure from simply being alive. We're so busy looking for the next carrot and the next carrot and the next carrot that we never have a chance to enjoy what we already have in our mouths (shades of our friend and his wild strawberries again!). Only when it's too late do we wake up to the fact that both in our childhood and in our professional lives we were so busy chasing future success that we lost somewhere along the way the ability to appreciate the present moment.

So take time off from your stress to sit down and appraise what is happening in your life, and what is good about it and what could be improved. Like giving yourself permission to have emotions, give yourself permission to have some time for yourself. Give yourself permission to stop feeling guilty just for 'loafing about' from time to time. If you can't let yourself loaf, use the same strategy as you did with emotions. Think back to childhood and those specific occasions when people urged you all the time to be 'busy' to 'find yourself something to do', to be purposeful and occupied, to think and plan ahead, to put off any chance of enjoyment now in the interests of enjoyment in some nebulous time in the future. That 'time in the future' is here now. All too soon it will be in the past. When do you start to live? 'Start to live', moreover, not by chasing wildly off after some idyllic holiday in the sun, but here and now, in the moment-by-moment experience that goes to make up being alive. Doing nothing special. Just abiding in the sense of being a unique individual, conscious of who you are and of what it feels like to be yourself.

Conclusion

I started this book by talking about stress in terms of the demands made upon us and of our adaptive capacity to respond. I hope that the things I've said since then will show that we can both alter these demands and alter those capacities. We aren't helpless in the grip of our stress. As I mentioned, 60 per cent of people who see themselves as stressed still admit to having no programme of any kind for dealing with it. They have missed the point that demands and capacities both lie to a significant measure within their own control. By looking closely at where their stress is coming from and at how they're responding to it, they can produce many of the changes that will render them better able to cope, and better able to enjoy both good psychological and good physical health.

No book on stress can be fully comprehensive. Each person is an individual, and experiences stress and stressors in his or her own individual way. But there are broad general guidelines that most people find helpful, and I hope I've covered most of them. They don't provide an easy answer. But in the light of present knowledge there *is* no easy answer. Making major changes (or sometimes even minor changes) in our lives requires effort, commitment, and often courage. It requires belief in the possibility of change, and belief in ourselves as people who can effect that change. And it requires patience and the realisation that this change isn't likely to happen overnight.

But in the case of stress, often this change isn't an optional extra. Our happiness and well-being (and sometimes our very lives) depend upon it. And when it comes, it brings with it not only an easing of the pressures under which we're trying to work, but potentially profound changes at the level of our personality and in the way in which we see and experience ourselves and other people. This isn't a bad goal to pursue. Except that in one sense it isn't a goal at all. It doesn't lie somewhere out in the future. It lies to a major extent in realising what is happening *now*, what it really means to be alive. Which brings me full circle back to our friend and his wild strawberries. He had the sense to realise they were there, and he had the tranquility of spirit to know that they tasted sweet.

KEY FOR PROFESSIONAL LIFE STRESS SCALE (see pages 22–23)

1. a) 0, b) 1, c) 2, d) 3, e) 4.
2. Score 1 for each 'yes' response
3. Score 0 for *more optimistic*, 1 for *about the same*, 2 for *less optimistic*
4. Score 0 for 'yes', 1 for 'no'
5. Score 0 for 'yes', 1 for 'no'
6. Score 0 for each 'yes' response, 1 for each 'no' response
7. Score 0 for 'yourself', 1 for 'someone else'
8. Score 2 for 'very upset', 1 for 'moderately upset', 0 for 'mildly upset'
9. Score 0 for 'often', 1 for 'sometimes', 2 for 'only occasionally'
10. Score 0 for 'no', 1 for 'yes'
11. Score 2 for 'habitually', 1 for 'sometimes', 0 for 'only very occasionally'
12. Score 0 for 'mostly', 1 for 'sometimes', 2 for 'hardly ever'
13. Score 0 for 'yes', 1 for 'no'
14. Score 0 for 'yes', 1 for 'no'
15. Score 0 for 'yes', 1 for 'no'
16. Score 2 for 'often', 1 for 'sometimes', 0 for 'very rarely'
17. Score 0 for 'most days', 1 for 'some days', 2 for 'hardly ever'
18. Score 0 for 'yes', 1 for 'no'
19. Score 0 for 'yes', 1 for 'no'
20. Score 1 for a), 0 for b)
21. Score 0 for 'exceeding your expectations', 1 for 'fulfilling your expectations', 2 for 'falling short of your expectations'
22. Score 0 for '5', 1 for '4' and so on down to 4 for '1'

INTERPRETING YOUR SCORE

As made clear in the text, scores on stress scales must be interpreted cautiously. There are so many variables which lie outside the scope of these scales but which influence the way in which we perceive and handle our stress, that two people with the same scores may experience themselves as under quite different levels of strain. Nevertheless, taken as no more than a guide, these scales can give us some useful information.

0–15 Stress isn't a problem in your life. This doesn't mean you have insufficient stress to keep yourself occupied and fulfilled. The scale is only designed to assess undesirable responses to stress.

16–30 This is a moderate range of stress for a busy professional person. It's nevertheless well worth looking at how it can reasonably be reduced.

31–45 Stress is clearly a problem, and the need for remedial action is apparent. The longer you work under this level of stress, the harder it often is to do something about it. There is a strong case for looking carefully at your professional life.

46–60 At these levels stress is a major problem, and something must be done without delay. You may be nearing the stage of exhaustion in the general adaptability syndrome. The pressure must be eased.

Index